JOHN DEERE
General-Purpose Tractors
1928-1953

Peter Letourneau

Motorbooks International
Publishers & Wholesalers

To the enthusiasts
who safeguard John Deere's legacy
of innovation
and superior craftsmanship

First published in 1993 by Motorbooks International Publishers & Wholesalers, PO Box 2, 729 Prospect Avenue, Osceola, WI 54020 USA

© Peter Letourneau, 1993

All rights reserved. With the exception of quoting brief passages for the purposes of review no part of this publication may be reproduced without prior written permission from the Publisher

Motorbooks International is a certified trademark, registered with the United States Patent Office

The information in this book is true and complete to the best of our knowledge. All recommendations are made without any guarantee on the part of the author or Publisher, who also disclaim any liability incurred in connection with the use of this data or specific details

We recognize that some words, model names and designations, for example, mentioned herein are the property of the trademark holder. We use them for identification purposes only. This is not an official publication

Motorbooks International books are also available at discounts in bulk quantity for industrial or sales-promotional use. For details write to Special Sales Manager at the Publisher's address

Library of Congress Cataloging-in-Publication Data
Letourneau, Peter A., 1950
    John Deere general purpose tractors, 1928-1953 / Peter A. Letourneau.
        p.   cm.
    Includes bibliographical references and index.
    ISBN 0-87938-723-8
    1. John Deere tractors—History.   2. Farm tractors—History.
    I. Title.
    TL232.5.L48   1993
    629.225—dc20   92-38246

On the front cover: The rare John Deere GP Tricycle, number 204,213, owned by Bruce and Walter Keller of Forest Junction, Wisconsin. *Peter Letourneau*

Printed and bound in the United States of America

Contents

Acknowledgments

Writing a history is a lonely business. It removes the author from friends and family for weeks at a time, and drives him into the dark and silent stacks of the libraries and archives that preserve the books, newspapers, journal articles, and photographs from which he draws.

Once the bits and pieces of the story are gathered, organized, and outlined, the author retreats to a corner where he writes, edits, and rewrites, and all the while he is scowling and mumbling and is generally unpleasant to be around. During this process, if the author is lucky—as I have been—he meets and interacts with people who encourage and advise him, and willingly provide him with photographs and anecdotes that bring life to the history he writes. If not for these people, history would never be written.

For this reason I wish to extend my sincere thanks to the following people: Les Stegh, Deere and Company archivist and gentleman; LeRoy Klein, founder of the Two-Cylinder Club, who was most generous with his time, knowledge, and suggestions; the staff of the University of Minnesota St. Paul Campus Central Library; the staff of the University of Nebraska Lincoln Tractor Test Laboratory, who have upheld the highest standards for over seventy years; Christine Schelshorn and Andy Kraushaar of the State Historical Society of Wisconsin, for their help; John Skarstad, curator, and his gracious staff at the Shields Library, Special Collections, University of California, Davis; the staff of the Henry Ford Museum in Dearborn,Michigan; Michael Dregni, editor in chief, and the crew at Motorbooks International; and finally, the Keller family, whose incredible foresight and dedication to John Deere equipment has yielded a wonderful collection of tractors.

On a more personal note, I wish to thank Tom Warth, who never wrote a book but inspired dozens of authors to do so; my parents, for the opportunities they have afforded me; my children, who sacrificed great chunks of our cherished time together; and, most of all, my wife Kathleen, whose precious love and faith in my abilities make my every effort worthwhile.

Introduction

Of the tens of hundreds of different tractor models manufactured in the United States since the early 1890s, few are as universally revered as those of Deere and Company.

This book is the story of John Deere general-purpose row-crop tractors built at the Waterloo, Iowa, tractor plant in the quarter century between 1928 and 1953. Included in this history are the Models GP, A, B, G, and H.

Powered by Deere's legendary two-cylinder horizontal gasoline engines, more than three-quarter of a million of these tractors were purchased and put to use on farms of all sizes. Sturdy, versatile, economical, and efficient, many were hard at work on a daily basis for decades.

While some of these tractors were never retired, most were relegated to a corner of the farm yard, sold as scrap, or traded for newer machines. Many were laid to rest in the graveyards of used tractor parts dealers. Abandoned, they were either dismembered for spare parts or left to deteriorate.

The American Heritage Dictionary defines an enthusiast as "a person who is intensely involved or preoccupied with a particular subject." It defines nostalgia as "a bittersweet longing for things, persons or situations of the past."

No one is more nostalgic than an antique tractor enthusiast and for that, we can all be thankful. Today, these Deere models enjoy a kind of "second life," due to the devotion of enthusiasts who have resurrected and restored, and who proudly display their tractors for others to marvel at and admire.

The development of the general-purpose tractor was but one step in the evolution of the farm tractor. The first chapter of this book summarizes the stages through which farm power progressed prior to the introduction of the general-purpose tractor. A review of this history will help the reader more fully appreciate the circumstances and demands that led to development of the general-purpose tractor, and to John Deere's entry into that market.

The second chapter is a chronology of the company's activities, from its beginnings through the purchase of Waterloo Gasoline Engine Company and the adoption of the Waterloo Boy tractor in 1918.

Deere's management acted indecisively and long postponed its decision to enter the tractor market. However, once tractor production began at Deere, the company proved itself as innovative and competitive as any other manufacturer.

Chapter 3 of the book encompasses the introduction and advancement of the general-purpose tractor, beginning with the motorized cultivator. This section focuses on the general-purpose tractor's importance as a tool for planting and cultivation, and its growth as a significant source of horsepower to a broad population of farmers.

The latter half of the book is devoted entirely to Deere's general-purpose tractors. The text, photographs, and illustrations included in this section relate the history of these fabulous green and yellow machines—machines that helped revolutionize agriculture and forever changed the way of life on North American farms.

Chapter 1

Heritage of the General-Purpose Tractor

While many features of Deere and Company's two-cylinder general-purpose tractors were innovative or distinctive, Deere was neither the first nor the only manufacturer of this type of tractor.

The generic term general-purpose was used throughout the industry and is synonymous with the terms all-purpose, universal, and row-crop. As the first term implies, a general-purpose tractor is one capable of all routine farm-power work, whether stationary or in the field. In particular, the term was introduced to distinguish a style of tractor whose design permitted its use in planting and cultivating row-crops (crops grown in evenly spaced rows, such as corn and cotton).

Early tractors were unable to operate in row-crops. Because of their weight and size, they were difficult to maneuver. Most had insufficient ground clearance to travel over young plants, as well as fixed wheel tread widths that prohibited their use in cultivating. As a result, even on farms with standard tractors, planting and cultivating row-crops was the work of draft horses or mules.

The story of the general-purpose tractor is a dramatic one. Its near-universal adoption facilitated the decline in farm labor requirements and fueled the growth in farm size. It boosted crop yields and made it easier for farmers to diversify their crops. Most significantly, the general-purpose tractor supplanted the horse and mule as the predominant source of horsepower.

The trade of "mechanical horsepower" for "horse" power began with the introduction of steam power, and accelerated following the development of the gasoline tractor. It was the versatile characteristics and affordable price of the general-purpose tractor that eventually put tractor power within reach of the average farmer.

Mechanization: Evolutionary, Not Revolutionary

The introduction of mechanical power into agriculture is often described as revolutionary in its significance on the farm industry. However, agriculture's mechanical revolution might be better described as evolutionary, in that mechanization and the advent of mechanical horsepower did not happen overnight, nor did it occur on all farms at once. From the first linking of steam power to a mechanized farm machine, it took American agriculture more than 125 years to reach a point at which the horse was no longer a practical source of power for every farmer.

Stationary Steam Power

Stationary steam power was the first step toward retiring the draft animal. In 1782, the Scot James Watt built the first steam engine to convert the back-and-forth motion of a piston into the rotary motion through which flywheels, cranks, and shafts could be turned. As early as 1786, steam power gained a toehold on American agriculture when Oliver Evans, a Vermont millwright, was granted a patent to build stationary steam engines to mill flour.

In his book *Steam Power on the American Farm,* Reynold M. Wik recounted the more direct early farm applications of steam power. Wik wrote of the first high-pressure steam threshing engine, which sold in England as early as 1812. Its inventor, Richard Trevithick, was so enthusiastic about the potential of steam that he wrote the Board of Agriculture stating, "It is my opinion that every part of agriculture might be performed by steam. Carrying manure for the land, ploughing, harrowing, sawing, reaping, thrashing and grinding, and all by the same machine . . . without the use of cattle."

In the United States, the earliest on-farm applications of steam power took place on the sugar plantations of the South. As early as 1808, Oliver Evans had shipped steam-powered mills to Louisiana for use in milling sugar cane. By the 1830s, several American companies were manufacturing steam-driven sugar mills.

Steam engines became an established source of power on sugar cane plantations. They proved invaluable to the large plantation owners who could afford them. On smaller holdings, cane farmers relied on custom millers, to whom they brought their cane for milling. By 1838, Southern plantation mills employed 31 percent of all stationary steam engines in the United States. By 1859, 75 percent of sugar plantations utilized steam power.

As significant a source of horsepower as steam engines were to Southern sugar cane growers, use of steam was negligible among the 2 million farms the US government recorded in 1860.

At this stage in its development, there were limitations to the use of steam that inhibited its wholesale adoption. The prohibitive cost of the steam engine was one of its major drawbacks. However, the greatest limitation of the stationary steam engine was the fact that it was just that—stationary. Large engines were installed on permanent foundations and often with roofs overhead. Without the means of locomotion, use of the steam engine was restricted to the site to which it was rooted.

Portable Steam Engines: Efficient Power For Threshers

In 1830, John and Hiram Pitts of Maine built the first practical threshing machine to separate chaff from grain. By 1860, the Pitts brothers' thresher was manufactured under license by more than fifty companies. According to historian Reynold Wik, the basic design of the thresher did not change for the next half century. What did change, however, were the thresher's size, capacity, and efficiency.

As threshers became larger, they also became more expensive to purchase and required more horses for power—the largest threshers required as many as fourteen horses. Few farmers could afford such a machine, and few had sufficient horses to supply the required power. As a result, it was usually necessary for several farmers to pool their money and animals to purchase and operate a thresher. In many cases, once their crops were harvested and threshed, thresher owners would do custom work, threshing their neighbors' crops.

It was these "custom threshers" who first made use of smaller steam units, in which a steam cylinder and flywheel were mounted directly to a boiler. Steam engines permitted threshers to be run at a constant speed. Such power units, small enough to be set on wagons and pulled by horse from farm to farm, made the efficiency of steam portable.

The development of a unit fitted to its own chassis and mounted on wheels was the obvious next step. In 1849, the first such portable farm

J. C. Hoadley's Portable Steam Engine, on Wheels.

Oxen, horses, or mules were used to draw portable steam engines. Self-propelled units followed in the 1870s.
Shields Library, University of California, Davis

steam engine, the Forty-Niner, was introduced. Available in 4, 10, and 30hp models, the Forty-Niner was not self-propelled. Like a portable unit set on a wagon, it was pulled by horse.

In his book *Fordson, Farmall, and Poppin' Johnny: A History of the Farm Tractor and Its Impact on America*, Robert C. Williams wrote, "The word portable as applied to early steam engines was a relative term. . . . When the thresherman finished his job at a farm, he had to prepare his 'portable' thresher engine for moving by removing various extensions and packing some parts away. In some cases, the boiler's smokestack had to be removed and stowed before a tongue and trees were attached so that a team of horses could drag the monster to the next farm. . . . While the horses attached to the engine strained and tugged, other teams were needed to move the separator, bundle wagons, water tank (and) coal wagon. . . . The delays involved in moving the heavy equipment cost the operator, tired his stock, and suggested that additional power was needed to move the steam engine."

By the outbreak of the Civil War, more than twenty companies manufactured farm steam engines. Included among the earliest manufacturers were Hoard and Bradford in 1850; Gaar Scott in 1852; Ames Iron Works in 1854; Robinson and Company in 1860; and Rumely in 1863.

Despite innovations and the increase in manufacture, steam engines were used primarily by custom threshers, and only on a handful of farms. In 1860, the average acreage of improved land per farm was less than eighty. The majority of farmers

Frick portable steam engine, circa 1875. The engine was manufactured by George Frick of Waynesboro, Pennsylvania. Smithsonian Institution

had neither sufficient cash nor animals to do much more than subsist, let alone hire someone to thresh their grain.

In the years following the Civil War, agricultural expansion created tremendous demands for machinery and steam power. Between 1860 and 1880, the number of farms in the United States doubled to more than 4 million. The number of improved acres increased from 163 to 285 million, a growth of 75 percent. This expansion was fueled by the offers of free or cheap land and facilitated by the expansion of the railroads. In these decades, millions of people were attracted to the upper midwestern and western states.

As the number of farms increased, so did the number of large-scale farms, especially in the wheat lands. Wheat acreage more than doubled between 1860 and 1880. As production surged, so did the demand for threshing equipment. More and larger machines were built, which necessitated more power than could be efficiently provided by draft animals. Thus, the opening for the portable steam engine.

Self-Propelled Steam Engine: Giant Step Toward The Modern Tractor

By the 1860s, knowledge of steam's capabilities and dreams of its potential were widespread. Among farmers, engineers, implement manufacturers, journalists, and politicians, the steam engine was a significant topic of interest throughout the years of its development.

The potential of a steam plow was recognized long before it was technologically feasible. Inventor Richard Trevithick wrote of it in 1812. In 1850 Horace Greeley, American journalist and politician, wrote, "The time must be at hand when every thrifty farmer will have [a steam] engine of his own. . . . This engine will be running on wheels and driving a scythe before it or drawing a plow behind it within five years."

In 1859, Abraham Lincoln addressed the Wisconsin State Agriculture Society, calling for a steam plow that could "plow better than can be done with animal power."

At this stage in its development, the portable steam engine was incapable of performing any function other than that of stationary work. It was still not a tractor. Dreams and endorsements aside, before the steam engine could truly perform field work, it had to be made self-propelling.

The self-propelled steam traction engine did, of course, become reality. When it was perfected, its primary market was with custom threshers who saw a benefit in not having to pull their unit with horses. However, some of the earliest examples of self-propelled steam traction engines were, in fact, intended for plowing.

In his book *The Agricultural Tractor: 1855—1950,* R. B. Gray wrote about the limited examples of self-propelled steam plows built in the 1850s and 1860s. None of these units was successful because of impractical drive systems and mammoth proportions. Also, most were built by individuals with inadequate capital to manufacture in practical quantities.

Gray wrote, "One of the first successful 'steam plows' [was] produced in the United States, by [Joseph] W. Fawkes, in 1858. The main frame of iron was 8ft wide by 12ft long and rested on the axle of a roller (driver) 6ft in diameter and 6ft wide. One cylinder 9in in diameter with 15in stroke was provided on each side of the boiler and the engine was so geared that the drive roller made one revolution to six strokes of the piston." The Fawkes tractor featured a 30hp Lancaster engine and upright boiler.

Following its demonstration at the 1858 Illinois State Fair, the performance of the Fawkes steam plow was reported in the *Chicago Press:*

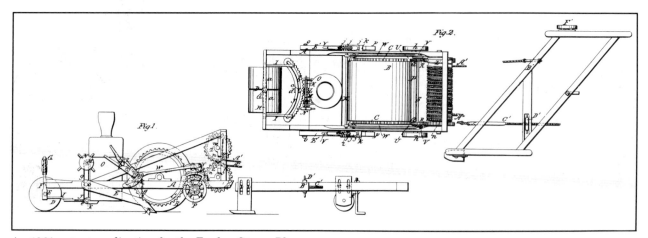

An 1861 patent application for the Fawkes Steam Plow.
Shields Library, University of California, Davis

"The excitement of the crowd was beyond control . . . beneath the smiling autumn sun lay the first furrow turned by steam on the broad prairies of the mighty West. The goal was won. Steam had conquered the face of nature and the steam plow had become a fact."

Enthusiasm for the Fawkes steam plow eventually waned, a common fate for early steam plows. Most were grandiose machines that proved impractical for plowing.

Wayne G. Broehl, Jr., author of *John Deere's Company: A History of Deere & Company and Its Times,* revealed that John Deere personally took an interest in steam plows. He built a plow that was pulled by a Fawkes steam engine. As tractors evolved, the company continued to design and build plows suited for use with tractors.

According to Broehl, in 1858 John Deere even ordered a steam engine built in Deere shops. Deere wrote a friend, "It will be a great day when Illinois can show a steam engine taking along a breaking plow, turning over a furrow 10 or 12ft in width as it goes."

It would be sixty years, however, before Deere and Company purchased Waterloo Gasoline Engine Company and entered into tractor production under its own name. Imagine how Deere's history as a tractor manufacturer might have developed had John Deere succeeded at introducing his steam engine.

By the mid-1870s, before practical self-propelled traction units were designed, a number of companies realized that rather than design a self-propelled unit from scratch, the easiest course would be to design a means to drive the existing style of portable engine.

More than one inventor devised a system of gearing a drive wheel, connected by chain or belt to a shaft driven off the engine flywheel. Thereafter, a variety of small portable engine manufacturers converted their existing units and began selling them as traction engines.

The principal builders of threshing machines were among the major portable engine manufacturers of this period. These companies entered the steam engine market as a complement to their core business. Initially, most saw little reason to enter this new market. They quickly took action, however, once the demand for steam traction proved genuine.

The earliest examples of steam traction engines were not self-steering. Instead, a horse was hitched to the front of the machine for that purpose. But mechanisms for steering were soon devised, as well as improved clutches and gear trains. By the late 1870s, the self-propelled and

A common scene well into the 1940s: a farmer, his lone horse, and a John Deere walking steel-beam plow. Deere Archives

self-steering portable steam engine took a giant step toward becoming a tractor.

The Steam Traction Engine

Sales of steam traction engines were highest in the wheat-growing regions of the upper midwest, western United States, and western Canadian provinces of Manitoba, Saskatchewan, and Alberta. For the most part traction engines were purchased by custom threshers, who furnished 90 percent of the steam power. This same group had purchased the bulk of stationary and portable steam engines. The new machines could provide sufficient horsepower to meet the ever-increasing demand of threshing, without the need of horses.

Farmers themselves had limited use for the stationary power steam provided, other than at harvest time. It was estimated that fewer than 5 percent of farmers operated steam engines. Yet the appeal of steam and the potential that it offered, as a source of unlimited, self-propelled mechanical power, again attracted farmers, engineers, and manufacturers to the notion of steam plowing.

Plowing requires more horsepower than any other demand placed on a tractor. Without tractors, that demand required tremendous numbers of draft animals in the large, open wheat fields of the United States and Canada.

As stated earlier, steam plowing had been attempted and had failed in the 1850s and 1860s. With the increased number of steam tractors being manufactured, several companies and individuals worked to reintroduce the steam plow. The steam tractor of the 1880s and 1890s had advanced considerably from that of the 1850s and 1860s. Yet, it was still not practical for plowing; a number of problems existed.

First, early steam traction units did not offer sufficient horsepower at the drawbar. Few could pull more than six plow bottoms, and they did so at a slow speed. Therefore, they offered little or no advantage over a team of horses.

Steam traction engine powering a threshing outfit; Russell County, Kansas, 1909. Smithsonian Institution

A second factor was that steam traction units were not intended for use as tractors, or "pullers." Their traction gearing was narrow and light-duty. They were not designed to withstand the strain of pulling a plow.

Despite their size and weight, the steam tractor's wheels were relatively small and narrow. Steam traction units bogged down in wet conditions and easily stalled on even moderate hills.

Another drawback was that the steam units were behemoth. Their size, poor turning radii, and lumbering nature made them absolutely impractical for turning at the headland.

Further, operating a steam tractor was never a one-person operation and despite the increase in production and competition among manufacturers, steam tractors were never inexpensive to purchase.

Other problems associated with using a steam plow included the fact that plows of the day were not designed to be pulled by a tractor, and were therefore not heavy enough to withstand the forces to which they were subjected. In addition, plows were towed by chains fixed to the drawbar. Without a hitch system, implements were difficult to manage.

Thus, the use of tractors for plowing by direct draft would have to wait for the smaller, more affordable, and more practical gasoline tractor yet to come.

Scope Of Steam Power's Success

In 1890, 3,000 steam traction engines were sold in the United States. In 1900, a total of 5,000 units were manufactured. In 1905, 7,500 steam tractors were built and by 1913, production peaked at 10,000 machines.

By 1920, the number of steam tractors sold had plummeted to 1,700, and in 1923 the J. I. Case Threshing Machine Company, which had built more steam traction engines than any other company, built their last steam engine.

For a relatively brief period, steam power was an essential source of farm horsepower. In the 1938 Federal Trade Commission's *Report of the Agricultural Implement and Machinery Industry: Concentration and Competitive Methods,* it was estimated that steam supplied 8 percent of power available on US farms in 1880; 10 percent in 1890; and 15 percent in 1900.

At its peak, in about 1910, the United States Department of Agriculture (USDA) estimated there were 72,000 steam engines in use on America's farms. That year steam supplied farmers with 3,600,000 potential horsepower, or 13 percent of the total available from animals, steam, and gasoline power sources.

The percentage of horsepower that steam supplied may not seem significant at face value.

Yet, it was. The "potential" horsepower available from animals was always substantially greater than that from steam. However, the "actual" horsepower supplied by animals was far less than its potential.

Animals required care, shelter, and feed, whether they worked or not. In its Bulletin No. 1348, the USDA estimated that animals that were used as horsepower sources required "the products from one-fourth of all crop land" as feed. The bulletin listed further disadvantages of animals, including their limited ability to work at heavy loads; rest period requirements; inefficiency in hot or sultry weather; limited working speed; inefficiency at stationary work; amount of time required to feed, harness, and care for; and large space required for shelter and feed storage.

By contrast, the bulletin listed the advantages of mechanical power as the ability to work continuously at heavy loads and without regard to temperature; excellence in stationary work; considerable range of working speeds; little attention required when not in use; lack of fuel required when not in use; quick availability when needed; and limited storage space required.

In considering the advantages of mechanical power, it was obvious that steam power offered far greater utility per unit of potential horsepower than did animal power.

Steam traction power arrived at a critical time in the growth of American agriculture—a period in which the demand for horsepower was crucial. Between 1870 and 1900, the cereal crop harvested in the United States increased from 1.4 billion bushels to more than 4.4 billion. Between 1870 and 1920, the number of farms and the total acreage from which crops were harvested more than doubled. In the same period, the population of the United States tripled. Without the efficient, unrelenting power of the steam engine, the supply of horsepower available to American farmers would have fallen far short of demand.

More than 175 US and Canadian companies built portable steam engines or steam tractors in the period between 1850 and 1930. Steam died a fast death, however, once the small gasoline engine became a more practical and efficient supplier of power. Yet, the development of the gasoline tractor would have been delayed for years, had it not been for the steam tractor.

As Wik wrote, "It was the steam engine that paved the way for the gasoline tractor and its development into the all-purpose farm machine of today. . . . It took 90 years to bring the agricultural steam engine to its highest point of efficiency. The tractor apparently took the same stride in less than half this time, thanks in large measure to the men who were trained in the school of steam-engine experience."

Enter Gasoline Power

The earliest work on developing an internal-combustion engine dates to 1680 when Christian Huygens, a Dutch astronomer and physicist, built a gun powder-fueled, internal-combustion, single-cylinder engine. Virtually no further work was done on the internal-combustion engine for the next 100 years as eighteenth century engineering was committed to the advancement of steam.

In the period between 1800 and 1860, a number of internal-combustion engines were built. None were successful. In 1876, the German Dr. N. A. Otto patented the first successful four-cycle engine design. His patent claims were so broad and basic in character that no one else could manufacture a gasoline engine.

Otto's patent rights expired in 1890. Soon afterward, many companies entered into production of gas engines. R. B. Gray wrote, "In 1899 there were approximately 100 firms in the manufacture of internal combustion engines in the United States; in 1911, 400 firms; and in 1914, 549 (not including automobile manufacturers)."

Early gasoline traction engine manufacturers had much in common. For the most part, their machines employed standard steam traction chassis and gearing. As with steam traction engines, these earliest tractors were designed as self-propelled, stationary power units and not engineered for field work.

Steam traction engine manufacturers were also drawn to the gasoline engine. They recognized its potential as a cleaner, more efficient, more reliable, and more economical power source. Gasoline engines had several advantages over steam engines. As identified by the USDA, they included:

- Efficiency: the internal combustion engine converted a greater percentage of the heat and energy value of its fuel into useful power
- Less weight per horsepower
- More compact
- Original cost was less per horsepower
- Easier and less time-consuming to start
- Less attention required while in operation
- Greater potential variety of sizes and types
- More easily adapted to a greater variety of uses

Almost from its introduction, manufacturers and engineers worked at improving the carburetion and ignition systems of the early gasoline engine, and at developing stronger, more reliable drivetrains. The first practical tractors, capable of field and stationary work, followed in the second period of development.

The Gasoline Tractor

The history of the gasoline farm tractor can be divided into five distinct periods of development, each of which was initiated or fostered by an innovative individual or company:

- 1889–1901: The Charter Gas Tractor and the years of experimentation
- 1902–1912: Hart-Parr and the proliferation of the heavyweight tractors
- 1913–1917: The Bull, the Cub, and the birth of the lightweight tractor
- 1918–1922: Henry Ford, Fordson, and the years of mass production
- 1923–Current: The Farmall and the years of the general-purpose tractor

Interspersed among these stages are the stories of the more than 800 American and Canadian companies that built tractors in the years beginning in 1889. Most companies failed, others merged their operations in order to survive, and a few took control of the industry.

Seven full- or long-line companies came to dominate the industry and are of principal importance to our story: International Harvester Company, John Deere Company, J. I. Case Threshing Machine Company, Oliver, Allis-Chalmers Manufacturing Company, Minneapolis-Moline, and Massey-Harris Company. By 1929, these companies held 96.3 percent of the total market share of tractors.

In just over thirty years, the gasoline tractor advanced from being a mere substitute for steam's stationary power to becoming the most critically important source of power on American farms—the general-purpose tractor. A summary of the four periods of development between 1889 and 1922 will set the stage for an in-depth review of the general-purpose tractor era.

1889–1901: The Years Of Experimentation
Charter Gas Tractor

Among tractor historians, there is some discussion as to who was first to design a successful gasoline tractor. By date of manufacture alone, the honor goes to the Charter Gas Engine Company of Sterling, Illinois.

In 1889, Charter built a tractor fitted with its own stationary-style, single-cylinder engine. The firm used a Rumely steam traction chassis. Six machines were built and shipped to farms in the Dakotas.

In his book *Encyclopedia of American Tractors,* C. H. Wendel wrote, "[John] Charter built and sold the first successful liquid fuel engine. [His] patent . . . was issued on September 20, 1887. Prior to this time, internal combustion engines used natural gas or producer gas for fuel. Through this patent, portable and traction engines became a possibility. Charter quickly adapted the gasoline engine to a steam traction engine chassis. [His] 1889 model was one of the first successful gasoline tractors."

In his book *Farm Tractors in Colour* Michael Williams wrote, "The [Charter] tractor was equipped with a reverse gear and with two massive flywheels to overcome the irregular running of the engine. . . . In spite of the limitations of exposed gears with primitive lubrication, the machine appears to have been a success. . . ."

Philip A. Wright, in his book *Old Farm Tractors,* gave us greater detail: "The gears were all open, of course, and mud and dirt (never absent from any form of farm work) simply played havoc with cast-iron wheels, which were not at all easy to lubricate. The gears wore out, in spite of the driver's great efforts to tend the primitive greasing-cups and wick-fed oil pockets which were the only lubrication given to the main bearings. The piston was equipped with 'sight-drip-oilers' [Gray refers to them as 'sight-feed oilers'] and the same lubrication even dealt with the connecting-rod bearings. The driver only had hard grease and a scraper with which he tried to inject lubricant into the teeth of the pinions."

Case Gas Tractor

In 1892, the J. I. Case Threshing Machine Company built its first gasoline tractor. It was the first attempt to build a gas tractor by an established steam traction manufacturer.

Powered by a two-cylinder opposed engine, its carburetor drew air through the fuel to pick up gasoline vapor before entering the engine. Michael Williams termed the carburetor system "notoriously inaccurate."

According to Gray, the ignition of the Case tractor was a crude "make-and-break" system, "whereby a bolt in the piston head contacted a stationary insulated electrode on compression stroke, and spark occurred just after dead center on outward stroke."

The engine was mounted on the wheels and frame of a Case steam traction engine. A sliding key was used to put the tractor gears into forward, reverse, or neutral position.

The Case gasoline traction engine was a failure, largely due to its unreliable carburetion and ignition systems. As a result, J. I. Case, the world's largest manufacturer of steam traction engines, dropped its gasoline-engine research. The fact that Case experimented with gas was significant. But, it was another twenty years before the company manufactured a gasoline-powered tractor.

Froelich Gas Tractor

The Froelich tractor is important to the history of John Deere general-purpose tractors. In 1888, employing a Case straw-burning steam tractor and Case 40x58in thresher, John H. Froelich began operations as a custom thresher. At some point, he realized that a gasoline engine would be a more practical power source than a steam engine.

In 1892, Froelich built what many believe was the first viable gasoline tractor, capable of both forward and rearward movement. On a Robinson chassis, Froelich mounted a single-cylinder, vertical-type engine built by the Van Duzen Gas and Gasoline Engine Company of Cincinnati, Ohio. Rated at 20hp, the engine had a 14 x 14in bore and stroke. The drive featured one forward and one reverse speed.

In the serialized article "The Engineer's History of the Farm Tractor" that appeared in the January 1967 issue of *Implement and Tractor,* Wayne H. Worthington, a mechanical engineer who joined Deere and Company in 1930, wrote, "[the Froelich tractor] was the first to incorporate the essential elements of a tractor: internal combustion engine, power train, clutch engaging and disengaging both, a reversing gear, manual steering gear and drawbar."

Froelich took the tractor to South Dakota that harvest season, to power and tow his separator. Over a period of fifty days, Froelich and his crew threshed tens of thousands of bushels of wheat. When he returned to Iowa, Froelich and three partners organized the Waterloo Gasoline Traction Engine Company to manufacture and market his tractor.

The company built four experimental versions in 1893. According to Broehl, two were sold but both were returned. When the tractor proved unsuccessful, the company turned to manufacturing stationary gasoline engines.

Froelich withdrew from the company and, in 1895, it was sold. Its name was changed to the Waterloo Gasoline Engine Company; the word "traction" was conspicuously absent from the new

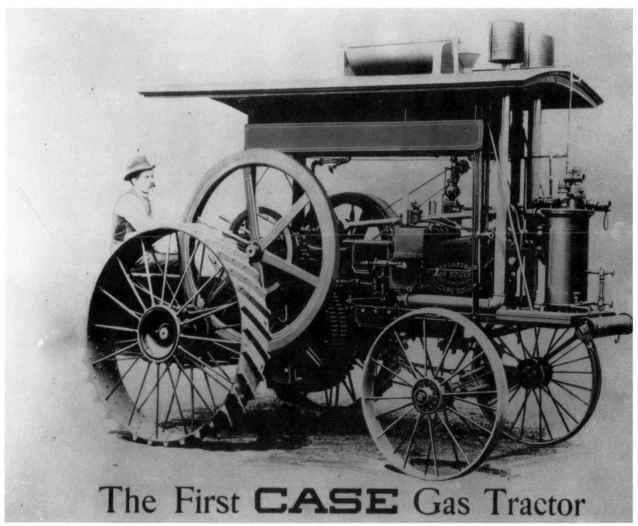

The First **CASE** Gas Tractor

J. I. Case, the leading steam traction engine manufacturer, built this gasoline-powered prototype in 1892. It never went into production. Smithsonian Institution

name. Except for two experimental tractors built in 1896 and 1897, the company stayed out of the tractor business until 1911. In 1912, Waterloo introduced its first successful tractor. The company went on to build several popular models. The Waterloo Boy name gained fame throughout North America, and in 1918, John Deere purchased the company as a means of entry into the tractor market.

1902–1912: Engine And Drivetrain Development
Hart-Parr: The First Production Tractor

While Charter, Case, and Froelich were among the first manufacturers of gasoline traction engines, none continued in production beyond the earliest period of experimentation.

The Hart-Parr Gasoline Engine Company is most often cited as the first to successfully mass-produce and market the gasoline tractor. The company is even credited with introducing the term "tractor" through its later advertisements.

Hart-Parr was innovative in its designs and aggressive at marketing. Its engine was oil cooled,

which permitted a higher temperature in the cylinder than if it had been water cooled. A hotter cylinder was beneficial in burning the low-grade fuels of the day. An oil-cooled engine was also less inclined to suffer frost damage, a consideration during midwestern winters.

It was, perhaps, to the firm's advantage that neither partner had been affiliated with steam engines or committed to the design of the earlier gasoline traction engine. From the start, Charles W. Hart and Charles H. Parr worked at developing a tractor capable of drawbar work.

Hart and Parr met at the University of Wisconsin in Madison. As engineering students they began experimental work with gasoline engine design, where they developed an oil-cooled, valve-in-head stationary engine. In 1897, while still students, they formed the Hart-Parr Gasoline Engine Company.

In 1900, reportedly unable to raise capital in Madison, the company moved to Charles City, Iowa, Hart's hometown. In 1901, Hart-Parr built its first tractor. The engine was a version of its

John Froelich built his first tractor in 1892. This is a page from the Waterloo Gasoline Traction Engine catalog, circa 1894. Deere Archives

16

Hart-Parr Gasoline Engine Company built the first commercially viable gasoline tractor. The company built this model, the 18-30, in 1903. Weighing 14,000lb, it was powered by a kerosene-burning, two-cylinder engine with bore and stroke of 10x13in. Smithsonian Institution

Kinnard-Haines Company, Minneapolis, Minnesota, built its first gasoline engine in 1897 and its first gasoline tractor in 1901. Shields Library, University of California, Davis

stationary engine and featured two cylinders with a 9 x 13in bore and stroke. It was rated at 30hp at the belt pulley and 17hp at the drawbar. The tractor's gearing was too light, however, for effective drawbar work.

Tractor number 1 was field tested during the 1902 season. Redesigned, the second Hart-Parr tractor appeared in 1903. The engine of this version operated at 280rpm and was rated at 45hp, with a drawbar rating of 22hp.

In production, the Model 22-45, as it was designated, featured heavier wheels and gearing. According to C. H. Wendel, it was the first Hart-Parr designed for traction work. Fifteen units were manufactured the first year.

Wendel quoted an advertisement for the Model 22-45, which appeared in 1903: "Perfect traction control forward or backward with a single lever. No shifting of gears, no water, no steam, no gauges. No fuels, no grate bars, no coal, wood, or straw. No fires, no fireman!"

Hart-Parr adapted various ignition and carburetion systems in the effort to improve its tractor's reliability. The Model 18-30 was introduced in 1903 and featured a make-and-break ignition system, powered by eight dry-cell batteries. In 1908, the firm introduced the Model 40-80, which featured a jump-spark ignition in place of the less reliable make-and-break system. The Model 30-60 or Old Reliable, as it was called, featured dual jump-spark ignition with low-tension magneto, two coils, and for starting only, dry cells.

Hart-Parr became the largest manufacturer of gasoline farm tractors in this earliest period of the production tractor. In 1907, it built one-third of the 600 tractors manufactured in the United States. By 1910, the company had sold a total of 2,000 tractors. Among the other major manufacturers to enter gasoline tractor production during this period were Kinnard-Haines, with its Flour City trademark, also in 1901; International Harvester in 1906; the Gas Traction Company, which merged with the Transit Thresher Company to build the Big Four in 1907 (among some Deere branch sales offices, the Big Four was a popular tractor that they sold prior to Deere's entry into the market); the Avery Company in 1909; J. I. Case in 1911; and, of course, Waterloo Gasoline Engine Company in 1912.

During this first decade of a new century, the expanding US agricultural economy encouraged both new and existing tractor manufacturers. In his book, Wayne Broehl quoted economist Harold F. Williamson: "The period from about 1898 to the World War I era has generally been regarded as one of exceptional stability and relative well-being for the American farmer." Production was up, while prices and income rose steadily.

The rise in income translated into more sales for implement manufacturers. Manufacturers saw substantial growth in sales as farmers increased their purchases of farm equipment. According to the Federal Trade Commission (FTC), the total value of agricultural implements manufactured in 1914 increased by 62 percent over 1899. By 1914, the industry ranked thirty-ninth among all industries in total value of products.

The new gasoline tractor benefited from this robust economic growth. Industry sales were reported at 2,000 tractors in 1909, and 4,000 in 1910. The gasoline tractor boom was under way.

By 1910, the year that steam tractor sales peaked, the gasoline tractor had become an acknowledged and significant source of horsepower. In that year, steam provided agriculture with 3.6 million horsepower. Gasoline power supplied approximately 2.3 million horsepower. By 1920, gas engines supplied over 10 million horsepower, compared with 3.5 million supplied by steam.

1913–1917: A Move To Smaller, Less-Expensive Tractors
Little Bull And Wallis Cub

Hart-Parr tractors, like many gasoline tractors of this early period, were gargantuan in size. The Old Reliable weighed 10 tons. Its flywheel, which was turned by hand to start the engine, weighed 1,000lb.

Despite their size, cost, and less-than-reliable nature, use of tractors spread beyond custom threshing operations. Although transformed to the gasoline plow, the century-old dream of a steam plow had become a reality. However, it was still only the large farm owner who could afford to buy a tractor.

In 1910, draft animals were, by far, the principal suppliers of horsepower, and there were more than 25 million horses and mules on America's farms. The horse would never have been replaced had it remained the most economical and efficient power source.

Hart-Parr and most others had designed their tractors to pull the multi-bottom plows needed to "bust" the prairie soils on large-scale farming operations. Tractor engineers now turned their attention toward designing lightweight tractors, to

Tractor Production and Sales 1912–1917

Year	Production	US sales	Export sales
1912	11,000	na	na
1913	7,000	na	na
1914	10,000	na	na
1915	21,000	na	na
1916	29,670	27,819	na
1917	62,742	49,504	14,854

Source: *Farm Implement News,* 1931.

meet the demand of the smaller grain and livestock farmers.

The period beginning about 1913 and ending with the emergence of Fordson, in 1917, was charged with innovation. With the onset of World War I, it was a tumultuous era for the gasoline tractor, the manufacturer, and the farmer as well. During this period, annual tractor production increased eightfold, from 7,000 tractors in 1913, to 62,742 in 1917.

The industry was growing. Yet it almost collapsed under the burden of surplus heavyweight tractors, which clearly did not meet the need of the majority of farmers. Production in 1913 fell 36 percent from that of 1912. Sales rebounded in 1914, however, largely due to the success of one tractor model—the Little Bull.

Little Bull

Introduced at the Minnesota State Fair in September 1913, the Little Bull tractor sold 3,800 units between April and December of the following year.

The story of the Little Bull illustrates the volatility that marked this epoch. It rose from a position of zero to 38 percent market share in just eight months; from first in sales in 1914, to seventh place in 1917, and finally, to suspension of production in 1918.

It was the demand for a small tractor at a reasonable price that inspired the Bull Tractor Company to develop and sell the lightweight tractor. The Little Bull featured a two-cylinder, opposed horizontal motor rated at 12hp at 150rpm. It transferred 5hp to the drawbar.

The tractor weighed 3,280lb. It had two rear wheels with drive to just one of them, which made a differential unnecessary, and a single front wheel. At a time when the Avery Model 8-16 sold at $900, the Little Bull retailed for $335 FOB Minneapolis.

Advertised as "the Bull with the Pull," the Little Bull was intended as a plowing tractor;

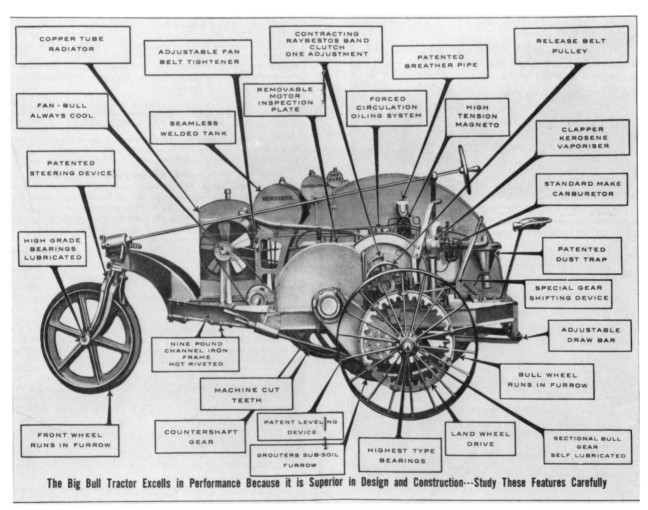

COPPER TUBE RADIATOR

ADJUSTABLE FAN BELT TIGHTENER

CONTRACTING RAYBESTOS BAND CLUTCH ONE ADJUSTMENT

PATENTED BREATHER PIPE

RELEASE BELT PULLEY

REMOVABLE MOTOR INSPECTION PLATE

FAN - BULL ALWAYS COOL

SEAMLESS WELDED TANK

FORCED CIRCULATION OILING SYSTEM

HIGH TENSION MAGNETO

CLAPPER KEROSENE VAPORISER

PATENTED STEERING DEVICE

STANDARD MAKE CARBURETOR

HIGH GRADE BEARINGS LUBRICATED

PATENTED DUST TRAP

SPECIAL GEAR SHIFTING DEVICE

NINE POUND CHANNEL IRON FRAME HOT RIVETED

ADJUSTABLE DRAW BAR

BULL WHEEL RUNS IN FURROW

MACHINE CUT TEETH

PATENT LEVELING DEVICE

FRONT WHEEL RUNS IN FURROW

COUNTERSHAFT GEAR

GROUTERS SUB-SOIL FURROW

HIGHEST TYPE BEARINGS

LAND WHEEL DRIVE

SECTIONAL BULL GEAR SELF LUBRICATED

The Big Bull Tractor Excells in Performance Because it is Superior in Design and Construction---Study These Features Carefully

The Bull Tractor Company, Minneapolis, built the Big Bull and Little Bull before production ceased in 1918. Toro, the company set up to supply Bull with gasoline engines, survives as a leading manufacturer of lawn and garden equipment. Shields Library, University of California, Davis

however, it lacked power. As noted, the tractor sold well initially. It had no competition to speak of in its price range. But its shortage of power, other design weaknesses, and production problems led to its early demise.

Although ultimately a failure, the Bull demonstrated the willingness—even eagerness—of the farmer to buy a small, low-priced tractor. In its Sixtieth Anniversary issue of July 9, 1942, *Farm Implement News* wrote, "The Bull tractor . . . sold in trainloads and proved that farmers were either power mad or plumb crazy about small tractors. Competitors wore down their molars tooth-gnashing about the Bull. Everything was wrong about it. . . ."

Competitors did take note. Massey-Harris selected Bull as supplier of its first tractor for the Canadian market. As Robert Williams wrote, "the iron ox's finest attribute was its price. . . . Cyrus McCormick, an official in the competing International Harvester Company, later summed up the little Bull tractor. 'It was never,' he wrote, 'a mechanically sound product, but its commercial popularity was such that it swept the field.'"

McCormick's own company, McCormick Harvesting Machine Company, which led the industry in sales from 1911 until the Bull charged onto the market, also entered into the lightweight division in 1914. International Harvester Company (IHC) sold more than 14,000 single-cylinder, two-plow Mogul 8-16 models between 1914 and 1917. The Titan 10-20, a larger but comparatively lightweight machine with a two-cylinder engine, made its debut in 1915. During its seven-year production run, 78,000 units were sold.

Wallis Cub

The design of the Wallis Cub was among the most innovative of this era. Introduced in 1913 by the Wallis Tractor Company, the Cub was the first tractor built without a distinct chassis.

Most steam traction engines and earlier gasoline tractors were built with a chassis constructed from straight or formed channel irons, to which separate components were bolted. This girder frame design facilitated the development of new tractors, as one component could be easily substituted for another. (This was not always a positive characteristic, however. With minimal engineering, a tractor could be built from off-the-shelf components—a chassis from one source, a gasoline engine from another. The final product was not necessarily a good one.)

The "Wallis Fuel-Save Tractor Cub."   Tractor "Cub" Economizador de Combustible, Marca Wallis

The principal advantages of the small Model "C" Cub Tractor are similar to those of the Model "B" Bear as may be seen from the illustrations on the opposite page. Perfect protection of working parts; easy accessibility; spring mounting; light weight and ease of operation. The "Cub" for its weight and price delivers more horse-power to the draw bar than any other tractor on the market. Its general specifications are:
Motor, 4 cylinder vertical, 6x7.
Diameter of crank shaft, 2¾ inches.
Length of crank shaft bearings, 26¼ inches.
Diameter of drive wheels , 5 feet.
Face of drive wheels, 20 inches.
Face of front wheel, 14 inches.
Width over all, 6 ft. 2 inches.
Height over all, 6 ft.
Wheel base, 8 ft. 4 inches.
Diameter belt pulley, 14 inches.
Transmission, 2 speed sliding gear selective type.
Weight, 8,500 lbs.
For complete illustrated catalogue showing all details and giving complete information of Wallis Fuel-Save Tractors, write (if interested),
H. H. WOODROUGH, Foreign Sales Manager,
No. 29 Broadway,
New York, N. Y., U. S. A.

Las principales ventajas del Tractor "Cub" Modelo C, son semejantes á las del Modelo B "Bear," según puede verse por el diseño de la página opuesta.   Las piezas de funcionamiento ván perfectamente protegidas, de facil accesibilidad, montado sobre resortes, de peso liviano, y facil funcionamiento. El Tractor "Cub" por su peso y precio, produce más fuerza motriz á la barra de tracción que cualquiera de los Tractores puestos hoy en el mercado.
Sus especificaciones generales son las signuientes:
Motor vertical de 4 cilindros, 6x7.
Diámetro del Eje de Cigüena 2¾ pulgs.
Largura de los Puntales del Eje de Cigüena 26¼ pulgs.
Diámetro de las Ruedas motrices 5 piés.
Superficie de las Ruedas motrices, 20 pulgs.
Superficie de la Rueda delantera, 14 pulgs.
Anchura total, 6 piés, 2 pulgs.
Altura sobre todo, 6 piés.
Base de la Rueda, 8 piés 4 pulgs.
Diámetro de la Polea de la Correa, 14 pulgs.
Armazón de transmisión, de tipo selecto de 2 marchas corredizas.
Peso, 8,500 lbs.

The Wallis Cub was built without a distinct frame.
Shields Library, University of California, Davis

The channel-iron chassis also contributed to the excessive weight of early tractors. The chassis itself was heavy, as it had to bear 100 percent of the weight of the components.

At the same time, little consideration was given to the weight or size of individual components. The flywheels and drive gears were often of massive proportions. Most transmission gears were of cast iron. Bulky chain was used with rollers for steering and to transmit power from engines to sprockets on final drives. At 8,350lb, the Wallis Cub outweighed the Little Bull.

Designed by Clarence Eason and Robert Hendrickson, the Cub featured a patented, U-shaped boiler-plate steel structure that served as the engine sump and transmission housing. In lieu of a chassis, it served as the backbone for the machine. Bolted to this structure were the engine block, radiator, tricycle front end (another innovation), final drive, sheet metal, and operator's seat. Not only was this structure rigid and strong, it also fully enclosed the transmission. All moving parts, with the exception of the pinion and ring gear final drives, were protected from dirt and moisture.

In 1916, the smaller and lighter Model J or Cub Junior was introduced. The Cub Junior featured the same U-shaped underbelly, extended to enclose the final drives. Its entire running gear ran in oil.

The Cub's design simplified its manufacture, but at $1,750, the tractor was expensive. Nevertheless, the Cub was popular and was recognized as one of the best manufactured tractors of its day.

The Wallis Tractor Company merged with J. I. Case Plow Works (not then affiliated with J. I. Case Threshing Machine Company) in 1919. In 1928, Massey-Harris purchased the Plow Works and carried on with the Wallis unit-frame construction into the 1940s.

Other Innovations From 1913–1917

In 1918, the USDA published the results of a survey of tractor operators who were asked about the weaknesses of their tractors. Ignition and carburetion systems were most often cited as problems. Nearly half of all respondents indicated a problem with either magnetos or spark plugs. Gear and bearing failures were also frequently mentioned.

R. B. Gray recounted a litany of problems responsible for ignition failures, which included "weak batteries, poor contact points, poorly insulated electrodes, weak magnets, damp spark coils, improper buzzer adjustments on vibrating coils, poorly insulated low and high tension wires and many other defects. . . ."

As the tractor industry matured, so did the quality of engineering practices. High-tension magneto ignitions with impulse starters and spark plugs were introduced about 1915. These develop-ments largely eliminated the earlier ignition troubles. Preignition, the untimely detonation of fuel in the engine cylinder, was a serious weakness of these early distillate fuel-burning engines.

In 1910, Rumely introduced a kerosene-burning tractor that featured a Secor-Higgins carburetor. The carburetor was fitted with a throttle governor that automatically controlled the injection of water into the mixture of fuel and air to effectively retard combustion.

Development of carburetion systems continued and by 1916, according to Wayne Worthington, improved carburetors "in combination with an intake manifold, intake passages, valve porting and combustion chamber configuration which produced high turbulence and swirl . . . effectively [controlled] 'preignition'. . . ."

Other period innovations that led to increased tractor reliability and performance included the introduction of hardened steel and hardened steel-alloy gears; improvements in and increased use of roller and ball bearings; enclosure of gear housings and transmission cases; reduction in the size of drive wheels; closed engine-cooling systems; pressurized engine lubrication; and improvements in air filtration systems.

1918–1922: Henry Ford And "Everyman's" Tractor

By 1917, the move to smaller, more affordable tractors was well under way. The Cub and Little Bull were only two of the more prominent lightweight tractors.

Even though the concept of lightweights had clearly emerged, in the industry as a whole, little—if any—consensus or standardization of design had been established.

Manufacturers used a multiplicity of designs and components. They included one-, two-, three-, and four-cylinder vertical engines; one- and two-cylinder horizontal engines; two- and four-cycle engines; transversely and parallel mounted engines; one-, two-, and three-forward speed transmissions; one-, two-, and four-wheel-drive systems; open and closed chain- and gear-driven final drives; live and fixed rear axles; and a variety of carburetion, lubrication, ignition, and air filtration systems.

The five-year period that preceded the introduction of the general-purpose tractor was marked by three significant events that largely forced an end to industry confusion. Those events were the introduction of the Fordson tractor in 1918; the recession that followed World War I; and the advent of the University of Nebraska tractor tests in 1920. The shakeup and shakeout that resulted from these events dramatically narrowed the number of manufacturers and focused the attention of those that remained on the demand for a low-priced, reliable, all-purpose tractor.

Henry Ford And The Fordson

Without question, Henry Ford was a genius. He established engineering, manufacturing, and marketing standards that set industry on end. Perhaps no other individual of twentieth century America was more responsible for the miracles of mass production and mass consumption.

Ford was born on his parent's farm near Dearborn, Michigan, in 1863. He spent a good part of his youth walking behind a plow pulled by a team of horses. That experience left an indelible impression. Ford was reported to have said, "I have walked many a weary mile behind a plow and I know all the drudgery of it," and "what a waste it is for a human being to spend hours and days behind a slowly moving team of horses."

While Ford's earliest commercial successes were with automobiles and trucks, he experimented with tractor design prior to the introduction of the Model T automobile.

His first prototype tractor, built in 1907, featured a four-cylinder Model B gasoline engine, as well as other automotive components from a Model K Ford. Transversely mounted on an automotive-like chassis, the engine developed 20hp. The tractor weighed only 1,500lb.

Ford built a number of tractor prototypes over the next decade. C. H. Wendel wrote that by 1916, Ford had spent $600,000 on tractor experimentation.

In 1915, Ford formed Henry Ford and Son and announced his plan to manufacture an inexpensive farm tractor, affordable to every farmer. Designed to pull two plows, he declared that the "Fordson" tractor would sell at around $200. Over the next year or so, a design was selected and fifty prototype tractors were built and tested.

The design chosen by Ford was largely the responsibility of Eugene Farkas, an engineer who

Henry Ford's 1907 prototype tractor. Henry Ford Museum and Greenfield Village

had worked on development of the Model T. Farkas proposed a short-wheelbase tractor without chassis.

As previously noted, the Wallis Cub was also built without a chassis. While markedly innovative, there were disadvantages to the Cub U-frame or unit-frame construction. One drawback was its manufacturing cost and another was its weight.

The Farkas design was compact, lightweight, and relatively inexpensive to manufacture when mass-produced. The tractor was built up from two stressed cast-iron components: a transmission and rear axle housing cast in one piece and bolted to a four-cylinder cast engine block. A cast front axle and steering support mount were bolted to the engine block.

The strength and rigidity of stressed cast iron (an iron and carbon alloy cast so as to withstand a specified force or stress) permitted construction of the first truly unitized structure without chassis.

Not only did the design make a chassis redundant, its simple three-piece bolt-together construction facilitated assembly-line manufacture—the keystone to mass production and a lower assembly cost.

Eventually, the Fordson unitized design became the industry norm and with few exceptions, modern farm tractors are still constructed in this manner.

World War I: Push For Production

Europe was already at war when Henry Ford announced his plans to enter tractor production. While the United States was not yet in the fight, the war had a decided impact on industrial and agricultural production, with reciprocal effects on both the general and farm-sector economies.

After the initial drop in trade at the war's outset, America's farmers were called upon to expand food production for export. Broehl wrote that in 1915, US wheat production hit 1 billion bushels, a level not reached again until World War II.

He added, "Commodity prices rose rapidly with general price inflation, and wholesale farm prices outpaced the 'all commodity' index in four of the five years of 1914 through 1918." Total farm income, which had averaged $5.9 billion in the period from 1910 through 1914, jumped 125 percent during the war years.

The call for increased food production, coupled with human-power and horsepower shortages, created a heavy demand for more farm tractors. In 1915, tractor production more than doubled that of 1914. At just under 30,000 units, production in 1916 almost tripled that of two years earlier.

The call for increased industrial and agricultural production was heightened when the

Henry Ford's personal Model T tractor/cultivator. Photo was taken in July 1915 on the Ten Eyck Farm in Dearborn, Michigan. Henry Ford Museum and Greenfield Village

United States entered the war in 1917. That year, US tractor sales increased by 78 percent over 1916, to a record 49,504 units.

Worthington referred to this period as a time of confusion for tractor manufacturers, and as a "heyday for promoters-turned-engineers." In 1917, eighty-five new manufacturers entered into tractor production.

Worthington wrote, "There was a spate of newcomers, with little trace of originality or sound engineering thinking in the lot. Component manufacturers boastfully hawked their wares—extravagantly claiming them so well developed that further field testing would be a waste of time. If one had misgivings at all, the ball and roller bearing people were ready with the latest scuttlebutt about what others were doing, and gave lavish assurances of experienced cooperation."

Cash Farm Income 1910–1918

Year	Cash farm income	Change from previous year
1910	$ 5,785,000,000	—
1911	5,581,000,000	–3.5%
1912	5,966,000,000	6.8
1913	6,251,000,000	4.8
1914	6,015,000,000	–3.8
1915	6,391,000,000	6.3
1916	7,755,000,000	21.3
1917	10,648,000,000	37.3
1918	13,464,000,000	26.4

Source: US Department of Agriculture, Bureau of Agricultural Economics.

In 1917, Ford came under pressure to accelerate production of the Fordson. The company was persuaded to initiate tractor manufacture by appeals from Perceval Perry, managing director of Ford's British operations.

In 1914, when war broke out in Europe, Perry assumed a position in the government and three years later became director of Agricultural Machinery. At that time, British tractor manufacturers faced material shortages that prevented them from meeting domestic demand. Perry turned to Henry Ford who agreed to build 7,000 tractors for export to England. With that commitment, the Fordson had been launched.

Ford was not the only US tractor manufacturer to export tractors to Europe in 1917. International Harvester exported more than 3,000 of its Titan 10-20 model. Waterloo Gasoline Engine Company, Case, and Wallis shipped tractors to Europe as well. Total US tractor production reached 62,742 units that year, of which 14,854 tractors were exported. In 1918, the closing year of the war, 36,351 tractors were exported.

Fordson Takes Control Of The Market

The production Fordson was fitted with a four-cylinder vertical engine. At 1000rpm, it was rated by Ford at 20 belt hp and 11 drawbar hp. The tractor featured a flywheel magneto and high-tension coils; splash lubrication; fully enclosed drivetrain in oil; automotive-type worm-gear final drive; and weighed approximately 2,700lb.

Fordson entered the North American market in 1918. At introduction, the tractor was priced at $750, and demand was both immediate and intense. In the first year of domestic distribution, Fordson produced 34,167 tractors and captured 26 percent share of the market.

By 1923, Fordson held 78 percent market share, when 102,000 units were sold. Through 1928, its last year of US production (production continued in Northern Ireland, however), approximately 750,000 Fordsons were manufactured.

The Fordson was not without design faults, though. Its flywheel magneto and high-tension coil ignition system were problematic, and made the tractor difficult to start. In combination, the trac-

The first production Fordson model built July 12, 1917.
Henry Ford Museum and Greenfield Village

tor's short wheelbase, worm-gear final drive, and high hitch sometimes resulted in instability under load. The Fordson was known to rear—the front wheels could literally lift off the ground—and there were reports of the tractor actually upending.

With regard to Fordson's performance under load, the short wheelbase, according to Robert Williams, "deprived the front of the tractor of leverage to counteract the torque of the rear wheels." As a result, the Fordson suffered poor transfer of power from engine to drawbar—a meager 6hp—and excessive rear wheel slippage of almost 24 percent.

The chart reveals both the positive and negative features of three machines: the Fordson, introduced in 1918 and produced through 1928; International Harvester's Titan 10-20, introduced in 1916 and produced through 1922, Fordson's nearest competitor throughout the 10-20 production run; and the Waterloo Boy Model N, introduced in 1917 and produced through 1924.

A statistical comparison of these tractors will not determine which was the better tractor. Facts, however, do point to the significance of the Fordson's success, and to the lasting impact of its principal design features. Consider the following facts:

• The Fordson overwhelmingly outsold its competition for almost a decade. It remains one of the best-selling tractors of all time.
• Fordson's unitized design enabled it to be more easily mass-produced, and cut its weight and material cost. It was widely imitated.
• Much of Fordson's success was due to Ford's ability to transfer manufacturing technology, as

Nearly 750,000 Fordsons were built in the ten years beginning in 1917. Shields Library, University of California, Davis

Tractor Feature Comparison

Feature	Fordson	Titan 10-20	Waterloo Boy Model N
Engine	Four-cylinder	Two-cylinder	Two-cylinder
Bore and stroke (in)	4x5	6½x8	6½x7
Rated load eng. hp	18.16	20.18	25.51
Rated load avg. rpm	993	577	771
Rated load drawbar hp	6.06	9.94	12.10
Max. load eng. hp	19.15	28.15	25.97
Max. load avg. rpm	1,014	580	724
Gears*	3 fwd./1 rev.	2 fwd./1 rev.	2 fwd./1 rev.
Final drive*	Worm-gear	Dble. chain/dead axle	Open spur gear & pinion
Rated load pull (lb)	1,472	1,827	1,982
Wheel slip (%)	23.80	11.70	11.84
Max. pull (lb/mph)	1,428/2.17	2,660/1.93	2,900/2.07
Construction type*	Unitized	Girder frame	Girder frame
Weight (lb)	2,710	5,708	6,183
Dimensions (ft, in; L x W*)	8'6"x5'2"	12'x5'	11'x6'
Price/Year*	$750/1918	$1,225/1918	$1,150/1917

Source: The 1920 Nebraska Test Results, unless indicated by an asterisk (*). Other data was supplied by manufacturers.

was employed in automobile manufacture, to tractor production.

- The rest of the industry was forced to follow suit. To remain price competitive, it adopted modern assembly-line methods and standardized and improved the quality of its components.
- Fordson's success clearly demonstrated that the farmer sought an inexpensive, small, agile tractor with a lightweight, modern engine and multi-speed transmission.

Sales of the Fordson greatly expanded the number of tractors in use. Census figures revealed 246,000 tractors on America's more than 6,400,000 farms in 1920. By 1925, the number of tractors reached 505,900, and in 1930 there were an estimated 920,000 tractors in use. Yet, even at the 1930 figure, fewer than 15 percent of America's farms employed tractors.

Although it sold well, the Fordson still did not fill the needs of the majority of farmers. Prior to the general-purpose concept, tractors—the Fordson included—were not an economical source of horsepower to most small farmers.

As late as 1935, over 60 percent of American farms were smaller than 100 acres. As Robert Williams wrote, "Tractors were incapable of invading the majority of farms until they could cultivate growing crops and work economically within the constrictions of undersized farms."

The Fordson was not a row-crop tractor. Nonetheless, it was a major step in the direction of the general-purpose tractor, and as Williams succinctly stated, "The competition that the Fordson stirred up eventually provided the motivation for developing a row-crop tractor. Then the success of the row-crop tractor encouraged innovative engineers toward the ultimate down-sizing of the tractor."

Nebraska Tractor Tests

Tractor comparisons had been popular as far back as the Winnipeg Motor Contest's Light Agricultural Motor Competitions, which ran from 1908 through 1913. However, a standardized and supervised testing of tractors did not exist prior to 1919.

In 1919, Ohio State University conducted tests of tractors pulling plows. The results were published and provided some useful comparisons. That same year, the Nebraska legislature enacted a tractor testing law whose effects still guide and influence the industry.

In an article that appeared in the February 1921 issue of *Agricultural Engineering,* Olaf W. Sjogren, then head of the Department of Agricultural Engineering, University of Nebraska, wrote, "The Nebraska Legislature was composed to a considerable extent of farmer members some of whom had purchased tractors that would not stand up or give them more than a few hours' service. The

bill [calling for tractor testing] was introduced by such a man . . . it is my recollection that it passed practically unanimously."

Sjogren continued with a description of the law's provisions: "(1) that stock tractor[s] of each model sold in the state be tested and passed upon by a board of three engineers in the employ of the state university; (2) that each company, dealer or individual who offered a tractor for sale in Nebraska must have a permit . . . to be issued after a stock model of that tractor has been tested . . . and the performance of the tractor compared with the claims made for it by the manufacturer, and (3) that a service station with a full supply of replacement parts for any model of tractor shall be maintained within the confines of the state. . . ."

A series of tests were developed to measure tractor performance under specific and standardized conditions. The first tests were carried out in 1920, and the results were published throughout the world.

Williams described some of what was discovered through these early years of Nebraska testing: "The tractors submitted in the first years of the Nebraska tests often had 'surprisingly major defects.' Testers found defective blocks, heads, valves, and other inferior parts. They also discovered that some tractors required excessive maintenance. Of the first 103 applications for testing, only sixty-eight appeared. The other thirty-five canceled their applications. Only thirty-nine tractors passed after major changes. The mechanical reliability (or lack thereof) reflected in the tests was roughly equivalent to the ratio indicated in literary sources of the time."

The Nebraska tests provided farmers with an objective measure of comparison. In addition, the tests accelerated tractor improvements and expedited the demise of a number of inferior models. Today, Nebraska test results remain the yardstick by which all tractor performance and manufacturers' claims are measured.

Postwar Recession

Cash farm income hit a record high of $14.436 billion in 1919, a level not achieved again until the early 1940s. The demand for tractors showed no sign of decline, as US sales soared by more than 41 percent over 1918, to a level of 136,162 units.

Demand eased in 1920, yet sales still grew by more than 19 percent to a level of 162,988 tractors. However, trade sales figures belied the actual state of the economy.

The economic growth spurred by World War I was suddenly and drastically reversed in 1920. Wholesale farm prices fell sharply, beginning a decline that was not reversed until 1924. Cash farm income slipped to $12.553 billion in 1920 and

Cash Farm Income 1919–1924

Year	Cash farm income	Change from previous year
1919	$14,436,000,000	7.2%
1920	12,553,000,000	−13.0
1921	8,107,000,000	−35.4
1922	8,518,000,000	5.0
1923	9,524,000,000	11.8
1924	10,150,000,000	6.6

Source: US Department of Agriculture, Bureau of Agricultural Economics.

Tractor Production and Sales 1918–1923

Year	Production	US sales	Export sales
1918	132,697	96,470	36,351
1919	164,950	132,162	19,693
1920	203,207	162,988	29,143
1921	73,198	na	na
1922	99,692	101,192	10,232
1923	134,590	117,701	16,643

Source: *Farm Implement News,* July 2, 1931.

plunged to $8.107 billion in 1921—a 44 percent decline from two years earlier.

The rate of farm bankrupties shot up by 260 percent in the period from 1918 to 1921, only to increase another 240 percent by 1924. Broehl commented, "For the very first time in the history of the United States, cropping acreage [declined]. By 1924, 13 million acres had reverted by default to grasslands, scrub brush, and woodland."

The collapse of the farm economy had dire consequences for the farm implement industry. In 1921, tractor production fell by 64 percent. Losses were heavy and the numbers of liquidations, bankruptcies, and mergers mounted.

The Federal Trade Commission reported a "sharp drop in [the] manufactured value of farm implements and machinery from $510,400,000 in 1920, to $192,875,036 in 1921 . . . to $146,967,028 in 1922."

Henry Ford Plays His Trump Card

Ford had made substantial profits from sales of the Model T, which permitted the company to extend millions of dollars in credit to its dealers during the postwar recession. But Ford also laid off thousands of assembly-plant workers, as well as cut production of automobiles.

In January 1921, Ford announced that the price of a Fordson would be cut from $785 to $620. A year later, in order to boost tractor sales and reduce material and finished inventories, the price of the Fordson was cut to an absurd price of $395. It was estimated that Ford lost at least $300 a tractor.

The decision to sell the Fordson at a loss brought hundreds of thousands of farmers into Ford dealerships—dealerships that were prepared to sell farmers cars and motortrucks, as well as tractors.

In 1922 Fordson sales, which had slipped from 67,000 units in 1920 to 36,793 units in 1921, rebounded to its 1920 sales level. Sales in 1923 reached 102,000 tractors, an incredible 80 percent of the 126,302 wheel tractors produced that year.

Ford's actions accelerated the industry's nose-dive, with fatal repercussions for much of its competition. Of the more than 180 companies that manufactured farm tractors in 1921, fewer than sixty were in production by 1925.

Ford And International Harvester Go Head-To-Head

International Harvester Company was created in 1902 from the merger of McCormick Harvesting Machine Company, Deering Harvester Company, Plano Manufacturing Company, Warder, Bushnell & Glessner Company, and Milwaukee Harvester Company.

From the moment of its creation, IHC was the principal US manufacturer of farm equipment. Its assets approached $110 million, and the five companies collectively manufactured 90 percent of the grain binders and 80 percent of the mowers sold in the United States.

Following the merger, IHC continued its expansion. It broadened its lines through conversion of existing plants, construction of new plants, and acquisition of a number of smaller companies.

In its 1938 industry investigation, the FTC reported that "by 1911 [International Harvester] became what was at that time regarded as a full-line company, manufacturing about 76 percent of the harvesting machines, 78 percent of the mowers, and 72 percent of the hay rakes. . . . [It] had also become an important competitive factor in the manufacture of plows, harrow, seeding machines, hay presses, manure spreaders, drills, hay loaders, side-delivery rakes, corn machinery, wagons, gasoline engines, tractors, motortrucks, cream separators, and binder twine."

In the book *Corporate Tragedy: The Agony of International Harvester Company,* Barbara Marsh revealed that by 1910 the company had spent $28 million on expansion, acquisition, and new product introductions. The investment paid off handsomely, as IHC sales grew from $55.7 million in 1905, to $101.2 million in 1910. In 1909, its assets exceeded $170 million and International Harvester became the fourth largest corporation in America.

International built its first tractor in 1906. By 1910, the company offered two lines of tractor. The Mogul line was sold through McCormick dealers and the Titan line through Deering dealers. In

1911, IHC took the lead in tractor sales from Hart-Parr. It held its dominant position until the emergence of the Little Bull in 1914; then recouped its position in 1915, only to lose it to Fordson three years later.

It was significant that Fordson, at this stage, was nothing more than a tractor manufacturer. Although Henry Ford had once announced his intention to offer Oliver plows and had even negotiated with Deere to supply a new plow matched to the Fordson, he had avoided selling implements. Ford also had avoided implement dealers. Instead, the Fordson was sold through Ford's existing automotive dealer network.

Henry Ford's competition in the farm equipment industry considered him an interloper. They regarded his decision to sell only tractors as evidence of his lack of commitment to the farmer.

To support its commitment to the farmer, IHC had invested heavily and worked diligently design-ing innovative tractors and matched implements. In 1921, the company could trace its roots in the implement business back ninety years. IHC management was not about to let Ford destroy its marketplace by a unilateral price war.

The Titan 10-20 was the Fordson's principal competition. Priced at $1,225 in 1918, its cost was reduced to $1,000 in response to the Fordson's January 1921 price cut. In March 1922, after the Fordson's price was slashed to $395, IHC lowered the price of the Model 10-20 to $700. To sweeten the deal, at that price the firm also included a three-bottom plow.

IHC Development Brings Innovation

It is unlikely that the reduced price of the Model 10-20 had any significant impact on Fordson sales. By March 1922, the 10-20 was an outdated tractor in its final months of production. More than likely, it was International Harvester's ongoing

The McCormick-Deering Model 15-30 ably fended off competition from Fordson. Shown here pulling a 15ft *harvester/thresher; Colorado, 1928.* Smithsonian Institution

28

effort at product development that eventually toppled the Fordson.

International Harvester management, led by its general manager Alexander Legge, had never overreacted to the threat from Fordson. The company had simply continued new tractor development, and with impressive results. In 1921, IHC introduced the Model 15-30 and in 1923 the new 10-20. Both models employed unit-frame construction, similar to that of the Wallis Cub. Its one-piece cast-iron frame ran from front to rear axle, and all gears, including final drives, were enclosed. As Wendel wrote, "Gone were the open drives, clutch pulleys and other crudities of earlier designs."

The 15-30 and 10-20 models were powered by four-cylinder engines. Both featured the first crankshafts to run on two ball-bearing main bearings, which substantially reduced maintenance and wear, and prolonged engine life.

These tractors were also the first designed with optional clutch-driven power takeoff (PTO). To anyone familiar with modern farm equipment, the significance of a PTO cannot be overstated.

Prior to the PTO, trailed implements such as the binder or mower were driven by bullwheels. A bullwheel was nothing more than a large, cleated wheel that rotated against the ground as it was pulled forward. Power was then transferred through a transmission on the drawn implement. The system had been used first with horse-drawn implements and it remained unchanged after the tractor was introduced.

Invented in France around 1905, the PTO provided the first means by which engine power could be directly applied to an operating mechanism while both the tractor and mechanism were in motion. As featured on the Model 10-20 and 15-30, the PTO was driven off the transmission. It featured a splined shaft, which, coupled to a matched connection on the drawn implement, rotated at a constant speed of 540rpm.

The comparative efficiency of the PTO was explained by W. Leland Zink, in an article that appeared in the February 1930 issue of *Agricultural Engineering*: "Tractor engine power can be applied to a drawn tool through the [PTO] with an efficiency of 80 percent or more. A 50 percent efficiency, however, is a high figure for applying power to the operating parts of a drawn tool when working through the tractor transmission and lugs back through the drawbar and drawn tool drive-wheels and transmission."

IHC engineers had the foresight to recognize the potential of a PTO. Along with these new tractor models, they also introduced new implements matched to each tractor and designed to be driven by power takeoff.

Within five years of its introduction, Zink found "power being applied in this manner to over twenty different types of drawn tools . . . also, [a PTO] attachment was being supplied for over forty different current and obsolete tractor models, or, in other words, practically every tractor built for agricultural use."

The 15-30 and 10-20 tractors were popular among farmers. The 15-30 remained in production through 1934, and more than 157,000 units were sold. The Model 10-20 was manufactured through 1939, by which time more than 215,000 units had been sold.

The 15-30 and 10-20 were just two of the three new tractors introduced by International in the early 1920s. The third model was called the Farmall.

Introduced in limited numbers in 1924, the Farmall was the first general-purpose tractor and to a large degree, its development resulted from Alexander Legge's efforts to displace the Fordson as the predominant tractor of the period.

The battle between International Harvester and Ford carried on until 1927, when IH regained its position as the leader in farm tractor sales. By 1928, US production of the Fordson had ceased. Manufacture continued in Northern Ireland, primarily for the UK market, and it was 1939 before another Ford tractor was built in America.

Chapter 2

Deere and Company: The Decades Before the Tractor

Eighty years passed from Deere and Company's origin as a one-person smithy to its position as a full-line farm equipment manufacturer. The tractor was among the last pieces of equipment added to the company's product line. Given its modern-day standing as North America's leader in tractor sales, it is ironic that Deere did not manufacture a tractor with its name on it before 1918.

Deere's policies toward tractor development and manufacture were influenced by several factors, which included the range of products the company offered, its organizational structure, and

John Deere and plow; painted by W. H. Hixton. Deere Archives

to a great degree, the competition it faced from the other full-line manufacturers that emerged in the first two decades of this century.

It All Began With A Plow: 1837–1842

John Deere, born on February 7, 1804, moved from Vermont to Grand Detour, Illinois, in 1837. A blacksmith by trade, Deere—like the farmers around him—was a pioneer.

As quoted in the June 1886 issue of *Farm Implement News*, his biographer wrote of Deere's earliest days in Grand Detour: "The settlers piled upon the floor of his shop broken trace chains and clevises, worn-out bull-tongues and worse worn shares, and, while the young blacksmith hammered out top-rings for chains, welded clevises, drew out bull-tongues and laid shares, his mind dwelt upon the improvement of the plow. . . ."

After a season of building iron plows with wooden moldboards, Deere experimented with different designs. The result was his first steel plow. Built following the farming season of 1837, its beam and handles were hewn from white oak rails, its landside and standard were forged from wrought-iron, and its share and moldboard were forged from steel, salvaged from the cutting blade of a local sawmill.

Deere reportedly built two steel plows that first year. In 1839 he built ten plows, and by 1842 his production reached 100 plows.

From his earliest days in business, John Deere believed in selling only the highest-quality plows. He continually sought improvements in both their design and material content. As a result, Deere and his plows soon earned a reputation for excellence.

Deere At Grand Detour Plow Company: 1843–1847

In 1843, Deere joined with Maj. Leonard Andrus to form the Grand Detour Plow Company. A two-story shop was erected, and in the first year 400 plows were built.

By 1847, the company built plows at the rate of 1,000 a year. That year, determined to relocate, Deere sold his interest in Grand Detour Plow to Andrus. (The company continued in business, and in 1919 was purchased by J. I. Case Threshing Machine Company.)

The restored blacksmith shop of John Deere at John Deere Historic Site, Grand Detour, Illinois. Deere Archives

John M. Gould, partner in Deere, Tate and Gould, and later principal in the Union Malleable Iron Company. Deere Archives

Stephen H. Velie married John Deere's daughter Emma in 1860. In 1863, Velie joined brother-in-law Charles Deere in the plow business. Deere Archives

Deere, Tate And Gould: 1848–1852

John Deere moved to Moline, Illinois, where he formed a new partnership with Robert N. Tate and John Gould. Tate had worked as a foreman for Grand Detour Plow. Gould, an accountant, had been a partner in a local department store.

In 1848, the first year of production at Deere, Tate and Gould, 700 plows were manufactured. By 1850, production reached 1,600 plows.

Gould's memoirs, quoted in the January 14, 1937, issue of *Farm Implement News*, revealed that Deere and Tate had several disagreements regarding "the manner of making plows." Gould wrote, "Mr. Deere wanted to make improvements all the time, while Mr. Tate did not believe in that; he thought that what was made was good enough. . . . Finally the trouble between Mr. Deere and Mr. Tate [became] so intense that Mr. Deere proposed to me that we have a dissolution. . . ."

John Deere Plow Company: 1853–1874

In 1852, the firm of Deere, Tate and Gould was dissolved and in 1853, John Deere continued his plow business without partners under the name of John Deere Plow Company. Over the next few years, as the territory in which he sold plows expanded, Deere enlarged the plow line to meet a variety of soil conditions.

By 1858, plow production reached 10,000 units. That same year, Deere took as partners his son Charles and son-in-law Stephen H. Velie.

In 1862, Deere and Company expanded its product line to include a cultivator, which was soon followed by a spike-tooth harrow.

In 1868, Deere and Company incorporated. John Deere retained 25 percent ownership in the corporation and was named president.

According to Don Macmillan and Russell Jones, authors of *John Deere Tractors and Equipment 1837–1959*, in its first year of operation "the company sold 41,133 plows, harrows and cultivators, with [sales] of $646,563."

In 1869, Charles Deere joined with Alvah Mansur to form Deere, Mansur and Company as a Deere and Company branch office, located in Kansas City, Missouri.

A second branch office was opened under the same name in St. Louis in 1874. (Its name was later changed to Mansur and Tebbetts Implement Company, following a break in the relationship with Deere and Company.)

The Gilpin Sulky: 1875

In 1874, Deere manufactured its first two- and three-bottom walking gang plows. That year, plow production at Deere hit 60,000 units.

Alvah Mansur, partner with Charles Deere in the plow business, corn planter business, and later in the first company branch office. Deere Archives

John Deere served as president of Deere and Company from 1869 until his death in 1886. Deere Archives

Deere and Company's extremely successful Gilpin sulky plow, with John Deere looking on. Deere Archives

Charles Deere, president of Deere and Company from the death of his father until his own death in 1907. Deere Archives

Deere introduced the Gilpin sulky plow in 1875. The riding plow had been introduced in the 1860s, and by 1873 there were sixteen different makes offered. Deere's version soon became America's second-best selling riding plow.

For fiscal year 1876–1877, Deere and Company sales reached $1,250,000.

The following year, production of corn planters began at Deere and Mansur, a manufacturing partnership formed in Moline by Charles Deere and Alvah Mansur. Also in 1877, a Des Moines branch office was organized under the name H. H. Sickles and Company.

By 1880, Deere and Company offered 180 types of plows.

In 1881, branch offices were added in Council Bluffs, Iowa, as Deere, Welles and Company, and in Minneapolis as Deere and Company (later changed to Deere and Webber Company).

Macmillan and Jones reported that Deere sales in 1883 included 48,858 walking plows, 7,841 riding plows, 13,818 spring cultivators, 9,198 shovel plows, and 14,604 harrows.

In 1886, John Deere died at the age of eighty-two. That year, almost fifty years after he had built his first steel plow, the company produced more than 120,000 plows.

The Minneapolis branch office of Deere and Webber Company was founded in 1881. Webber was the son of Charles Deere's brother-in-law. Deere Archives

John Deere held a position in the industry that went beyond that of mere pioneer. Broehl wrote, "[John Deere had] a knack for organization, an abiding concern for quality, and a feeling for the role of the agricultural equipment industry in America's growth, that made him a preeminent producer and distributor of farm machinery."

Charles Deere Years: 1886–1907

Charles Deere became president of Deere and Company upon his father's death. Appointed general manager in 1868, he had always held a position of leadership. In fact, Broehl revealed that Charles' father's role in the company had been "minimal after the Civil War."

Charles Deere had a keen sense of marketing and, like his father, recognized the importance of offering innovative and well-made implements.

Charles Deere is remembered for two critical accomplishments: the development of the branch office network, and the expansion of Deere and Company's product line at a time of rapid industry growth.

Deere formed local partnerships to build and expand the branch office network. He cultivated marketing agreements with a series of carefully chosen partners who manufactured products that complemented the Deere line.

These alliances permitted the company to offer a broad range of equipment to an expanded territory, and in doing so, greatly enhanced Deere and Company's position in the industry.

The Kansas City branch office of Deere, Mansur and Company was opened in 1869, and was the first of what became a coast-to-coast network of branch offices owned by Deere and local partners. It was through these branches that Deere and Company distributed equipment to its dealers.

As noted, branch offices were opened at St. Louis in 1874, Des Moines in 1877, Council Bluffs in 1881, and Minneapolis in 1881. The San Francisco branch opened in 1889, as Deere Implement Company.

By the time of Charles Deere's death in 1907, the company had opened fifteen branch offices (all but two west of the Appalachians).

By the 1870s, corn production in the United States was on the rise. Production hit one billion bushels for the first time in 1870, an increase of 190 percent since 1840.

As a feed crop, corn was of greatest significance to the farmers in the East, and in the

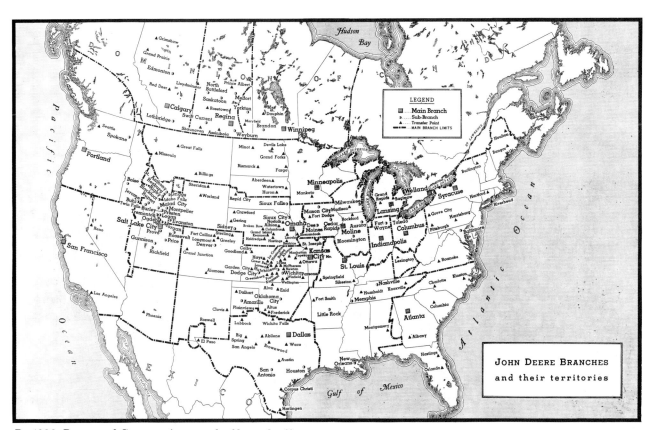

By 1938, Deere and Company's network of branch offices and transfer points spanned the breadth of Canada and the United States. Farm Implement News

Midwest region where Deere and Company was an established name.

In 1877, Charles Deere and Alvah Mansur organized the Deere and Mansur Company to build corn planters. Independent of Deere and Company, this was the first manufacturing partnership formed by Charles Deere.

Deere and Mansur's original planter evolved into the Model 999 which, according to *Farm Implement News,* "was quickly recognized by farmers the country over for its accuracy and dependability."

Throughout the 1880s and into the first decade of the new century, Deere and Company continued to build volume by offering products purchased from outside manufacturers. These included farm wagons built by Moline Wagon Company (which owned one-third share in the Council Bluffs branch office of Deere, Welles and Company); buggies built by Mansur and Tebbetts Carriage Company; harnesses manufactured by Velie Saddlery Company; grain drills built by Van Brunt Manufacturing Company; sweep rakes and stackers built by Dain Manufacturing Company; the Success manure spreader built by Kemp and Burpee Manufacturing Company; and a corn sheller and line of grain elevators manufactured by the Marseilles Company.

In an industry that included numerous short-line, regional firms, Charles Deere's two-pronged expansion of the company was of critical significance.

An August 1936 *Fortune* magazine article titled "Deere & Co.," said, "Charles opened the first of Deere's branch selling houses in the [70s]. . . . On these branches Charles built a distributing system that was soon the envy of the industry. Abandoning commissions, he sold plows to his dealers outright, so that instead of agents they became independent village merchants. In this way Deere & Co. not only made itself and its products seem more native to each farming region, but became the first implement manufacturer to recognize the importance of the 'full-line.'"

Charles Deere's half-century of leadership set the stage for a major reorganization and expansion of the company, which was not fully completed until after his death.

Deere And Company Grows with the Industry

As noted, the period from 1870 until 1920 was one of growth and relative prosperity for America's farmers. In 1870, there were 2,659,985 farms in the United States. By 1920, the number had reached 6,448,343 farms.

The farm equipment industry grew as the number of acres in production soared and new types of machinery were introduced. In 1869, according to the United States Census Bureau, the

A series of bullwheels drove this Van Brunt horse-drawn press drill. Founded in 1861, the company was purchased by Deere and Co. in 1911. Deere Archives

Deere and Company Sales 1899 Versus 1909

Product	1899	1909
Small cultivators	207,171	469,696
Wheeled cultivators	295,799	435,429
Disk harrows	97,261	193,000
Other harrows	380,259	507,820
Disk plows	17,345	22,132
Shovel plows	103,320	245,737
Steam plows	207	2,355
Wheel (sulky) plows	135,102	134,936
Walking plows	819,022	1,116,000

Source: *John Deere Tractors and Equipment 1837-1959.*

Growth in Manufacture of Agricultural Implements 1869–1914

Year	Number of manufacturers	Capital invested	Product value
1869	2,076	$ 34,834,600	$ 52,066,875
1879	1,943	62,109,668	68,640,486
1889	910	145,313,997	81,271,651
1899	715	157,707,951	101,207,428
1904	648	196,740,700	112,007,344
1909	640	256,281,000	146,329,268
1914	601	338,531,673	164,086,835

Source: US Census Bureau.

total value of farm equipment manufactured was $52,066,875. By 1899, the value had almost doubled, and by 1914 it reached $164,086,835. By the end of the nineteenth century, Deere and Company was the largest US manufacturer of tillage tools. Its sales for fiscal year 1899–1900 hit $2,144,570.

As Macmillan reveals in the chart, the company's sales of plows, cultivators, and harrows grew handsomely through the first decade of the twentieth century.

As the farm equipment industry grew and competition intensified, the capital required to manufacture, sell, service, and finance farm equipment grew at a rate far greater than that of sales.

Consequently, the number of manufacturers in the industry declined dramatically. Many companies merged, others simply disappeared. The nearby table shows industry changes for the period between 1869 and 1914.

William Butterworth: Reorganization And Expansion 1907–1928

In 1907, William Butterworth succeeded his father-in-law, Charles Deere, as president of Deere and Company. Five years earlier, in 1902, International Harvester was created from the merger of the five largest US manufacturers of harvesting machinery.

As previously noted, IHC invested heavily in plant expansion, in the acquisition of a number of smaller farm equipment companies, and in its own program of product development. As a result, by 1910 International Harvester offered a greater variety of equipment than did Deere and Company.

Butterworth and Deere directors were acutely aware that International Harvester's dominance of the industry would one day threaten their company's position as leader in tillage equipment sales.

Moreover, it was apparent that for Deere to continue to prosper, the company would have to firmly establish its position as a full- or long-line manufacturer. To meet the challenge posed by

International and others, the directors met on January 6, 1910, and empowered a committee of five to "formulate a plan of re-organization."

Appointed by Butterworth, the committee focused on a number of issues that included complete integration of the branch sales offices, most of which had remained at least partially owned by the original local partners; "unification" of the allied manufacturers, who either supplied components to Deere's factories or finished units that were sold through Deere's branches; further enlargement of the product line to include harvest-

William Butterworth, company president from 1907 to 1928. Butterworth was the son-in-law of Charles Deere.
Deere Archives

Union Malleable Iron Company, circa 1898. Deere Archives

called Deere and Company) for the purpose of buying out all local branch office partners and allied suppliers. The acquired companies were to be merged with Deere's existing business and would operate under the new company's management.

The plan was instituted, and over the next two years the company brought under its control all of the branches: Deere and Mansur; Kemp and Burpee; Van Brunt Manufacturing; Fort Smith Wagon (acquired in 1907, but run independently until 1911); Deere, Welles and Company ; Union Malleable Iron Company, which produced chain and iron castings for Deere; Dain Manufacturing; and Marseilles Company.

Also in 1911, the company acquired Syracuse Chilled Plow Company. Although Deere already built a chilled plow, the Syracuse plow was considered to be more competitive with that of Oliver.

Deere Adds Harvesting Equipment

Following the effective integration of its former partners, Deere's management turned its attention to harvesting equipment. Since 1902, this facet of the industry had been dominated by International Harvester.

In 1909, unable to purchase an existing manufacturer whose product line was competitive with

ing equipment; and a financial and structural reorganization that would permit a successful integration and expansion program.

Acting on the advice of the committee, the decision was made to form a holding company (also

The name Van Brunt figured prominently in this Deere advertisement for grain drills. Deere Archives

that of IHC, Deere's board approved in-house development of a binder.

As Macmillan related, over the next two years the company developed a successful prototype binder and eventually built 500 units. Joseph Dain took charge of the operation in late 1911, and through the winter and spring of 1912, 2,000 binders were built.

Firmly committed to this new line, the board approved construction of a production facility devoted to harvesting equipment. A factory, foundry, and warehouse complex named the Harvester Works was built in East Moline, Illinois, during 1912 and 1913. In 1914, its first year of operation, the new factory turned out 12,000 harvesters.

Deere Turns Its Attention to Tractors: 1912–1918

By 1910 the gasoline tractor had become a significant source of horsepower to America's farmers. From the earliest days of the steam plow, Deere and Company management had kept a watchful eye on tractor development. However, it did so from the perspective of an implement builder and not from that of a prospective tractor manufacturer.

It was 1912, more than sixty years following the introduction of the first practical portable steam engines, before Deere management gave its first serious consideration to tractor development.

According to Wayne Broehl, at a directors' meeting in March 1912, the board passed a resolution that stated, "In view of the inevitable future use by farmers for diverse purposes of gasoline and kerosene tractors . . . a movement to produce a tractor plow should be started at once. . . ."

While the resolution passed unanimously, Broehl's study of future board minutes and company correspondence revealed the division that actually existed in management regarding the question of a Deere tractor.

Broehl studied William Butterworth's private notes, written sometime in 1912, and revealed that "Butterworth laid out four tightly packed pages of handwritten thoughts concerning management problems and possible cost-cutting efforts within the company."

Broehl continued, "The last page concluded with a set of comments on over-all 'economic policy'[:] 'buy carefully; manufacture under slow bill; reduce our large inventory by converting into cash; reduce our bank loan as much as possible, [and] spend no money for any kind of expansion beyond our present Harvester addition and the Foundry.'

"Finally, he appended one more line—the last line in the entire memorandum: 'drop all tractor expenditures.'"

As it turned out, an experimental tractor was built but was a failure. Broehl wrote, "By the spring of 1914 all further work [on a tractor] was halted."

For several reasons, it is not difficult to understand the conservative approach taken by Deere management with regard to tractor production. Consider the following factors.

First, not everyone in the industry was convinced that the tractor would ever be widely adopted.

In 1912, the Harvester Works were built in East Moline, Illinois. Deere Archives

Although Deere did not build a tractor before 1918, the company did build plows suited to steam traction en- *gines. Here is a ten-bottom Deere gang plow and Case steam traction engine, circa 1907.* Deere Archives

The Melvin experimental tractor, 1912—the company's first effort at building a tractor. Deere Archives

Second, prior to 1900, portable steam and gasoline engines were used principally as stationary power units. The primary buyers used their power to drive threshing machines.

For the most part, the tractor industry developed among the threshing equipment builders—who viewed steam and gasoline traction engines as the logical extension of their existing businesses—

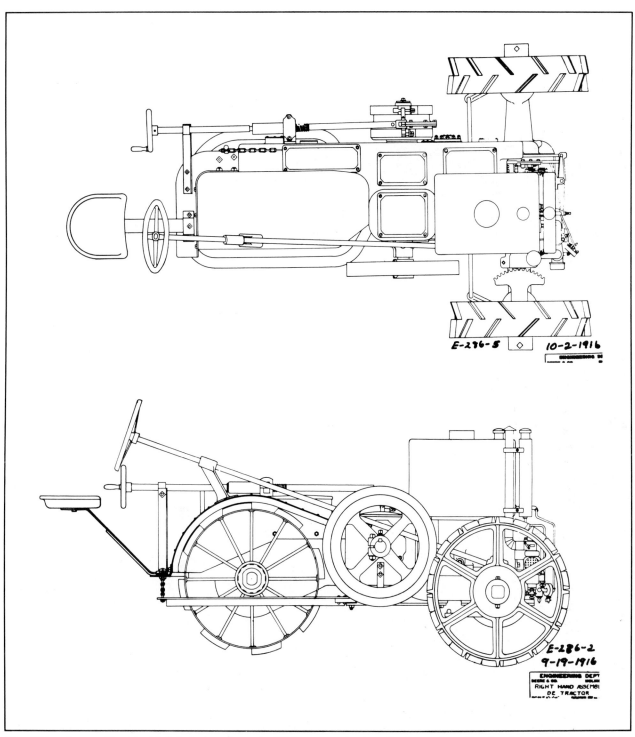

Max Sklovsky was Deere's chief design engineer in 1915, when he developed a prototype two-plow tractor. Originally designated the Model A-2, it was rebuilt as the Model B-2. A third design, the Model D-2, featured a single-cylinder engine. Overhead and side views of the D-2 are depicted in this engineering drawing, dated September 1916. Deere Archives

and among the engine manufacturers themselves. Deere and Company had no interest in threshing equipment, nor did it build steam or gasoline engines.

A third factor was that prior to the introduction of the Hart-Parr tractor, little practical consideration had been given to the demands placed on an implement when pulled by a steam or gasoline traction engine.

As *Fortune* magazine wrote, "the very fact of the tractor gave Deere more to think about than the demand for it." Implements had to be redesigned and the challenges faced by Deere included the differences in the line of draft (the angle at which an implement was pulled) which, with a horse, sloped upward from the plow bottom to the horse's shoulders; with a tractor, the draft was almost horizontal to the drawbar. Other needs included a means to lift implements over obstructions, while the tractor and implement were in movement; the greater and steadier force exerted by a tractor, which demanded a heavier implement; and the greater cost associated with such revisions.

Joseph Dain, Sr., was charged with building Deere's last experimental tractor, prior to purchase of Waterloo Boy. Dain died unexpectedly, but 100 units of his tractor were built in 1917. Deere Archives

The state of the art in tractor manufacture was very much in flux, even into the 1920s. The various designs of engines, ignition systems, carburetors, air filters, cooling and exhaust systems, transmissions, final drives, brakes, and so on, confounded even the most experienced mechanical engineers. It was not possible for Deere to simply "build" a tractor without considerable investment of time, personnel, and money.

From the standpoints of logistics and cost, the reorganization and expansion of 1910–1912 was a mammoth undertaking that preoccupied Deere management.

Another factor influencing Deere's conservative approach was that the decentralized structure of the organization left many management responsibilities in the hands of factory and branch managers. Central management was left to the president, an executive committee, and the board of directors. A major undertaking like the tractor was not something readily accepted by this diverse group of individuals and interests.

In addition, to execute the reorganization, integration, and harvester expansion programs, Deere had taken on new shareholders (principally, the former owners of the acquired companies and branches) and increased its bank debt. Butterworth, in particular, was concerned that an expenditure on tractor development would be viewed as imprudent by shareholders and bankers.

Finally, the onset of World War I diverted interest from tractors, as Deere sales and profits were severely reduced in 1914.

In retrospect, Deere's cautious approach to tractor development is understandable, given all that occurred between 1900 and 1915—at Deere and Company, in the agricultural economy, and within the farm equipment industry.

The years of World War I were marked by a heightened demand for farm equipment, brought about by the call for increased food production. Agricultural commodity prices increased an average of 118 percent, and cash farm income jumped 125 percent during the same period.

The total value of farm equipment sold in the United States increased from $164,086,835 in 1914 to $304,961,265 in 1919. While a portion of that increase resulted from inflationary pressures, real growth through the war years was reflected in tractor sales which exceeded 325,000 units.

Active Tractor Development At Deere: 1915–1918

By 1915, profits rebounded at Deere. While overall sales declined, the harvester line turned its first profit, the company's operating costs were reduced, and overall inventories were lowered. Sales remained flat through 1916, but profits continued to climb—up 130 percent over 1914.

Side view of Dain all-wheel-drive tractor, photographed inside the factory. Note the single rear wheel and chain drives. Deere Archives

All-wheel-drive Dain tractor drawing a breaker plow, circa 1919. Deere Archives

Willard L. Velie, a long-time member of Deere's board, circa 1910. Deere Archives

The growth in tractor sales did not go unnoticed among Deere management, branch personnel, and dealers. Broehl wrote that in 1915 Ralph Lourie, a board member and Moline branch manager, again raised the issue of producing a tractor. Lourie perceived a threat to Deere's implement business as, in his words, "the tractor people [were] selling plows right on their tractors."

Earlier in 1915 the company had authorized a market study of the situation, which led to the construction of a new prototype tractor. Built under the direction of Joseph Dain and tested through the summers of 1915 and 1916, the prototype featured all-wheel-drive. The chain-driven, three-wheeled tractor was rated at 24 engine and 12 drawbar hp. It pulled a three-bottom plow.

Also in 1915, the board approved experimentation with motorized cultivators and the development of a third prototype tractor, both under the direction of Max Sklovsky, Deere's chief engineer.

In spite of this activity, the question of tractor production remained a divisive issue among board members. Butterworth remained adamantly opposed to a Deere-built tractor.

In a September 1916 letter he cited his reasons for opposition, which included his belief that tractor development was a waste of stockholders' money; his reluctance to go head-to-head with Henry Ford who, with "unlimited capital and resources," had recently declared his intention to build a tractor; and his opinion that the company should have been, in fact, "reducing [its] line rather than expanding it."

Another year passed before a decision was finally made regarding the Dain tractor. In September 1917, the board approved production of 100 units. Soon afterward, Dain died unexpectedly.

Following Dain's death, Willard L. Velie attempted to force the board to make a deeper commitment to tractor production. Velie wrote each member and reminded them that they had unanimously approved building a tractor in March 1912. As he pointed out, Deere had spent $250,000 on tractor experimentation but had progressed no further than the recent approval of a limited number of Dain tractors.

It was Velie's opinion that the company could not afford to build as few as 100 tractors. Such a move would do little more than put Deere into competition with the numerous independent tractor manufacturers, which had, in Velie's words, "been heretofore our allies." He concluded his letter by stating that the company should either build tractors, "largely and whole-heartedly, or dismiss the tractor matter as inconsequential and immaterial."

Velie was not alone in his opinion. To the majority of board members, it was clear that Deere could no longer afford to sit on the fence. Not only were tractor sales booming, but more than one competing plow manufacturer had started to build tractors. Furthermore, reports from the field indicated that Deere dealers perceived their plow business to be in jeopardy because Deere and Company did not offer a tractor.

Finally, in January 1918, the board was prepared to act. However, the direction took a new turn when Frank Silloway, a board member and then sales manager, suggested that rather than continue in-house development, the company consider the purchase of Waterloo Gasoline Engine Company, manufacturer of the Waterloo Boy tractor.

Waterloo Boy Joins The Fold

Silloway's proposal was met with interest. The company acted quickly, once a review of the records and facilities of Waterloo Gasoline Engine Company was completed.

The board was overwhelmingly impressed with Waterloo Gasoline's modern factory in Waterloo, Iowa, and was satisfied with the performance and retail price of the Waterloo Boy tractor. It was Silloway's opinion that, in terms of popularity, Waterloo Boy was second only to International Harvester tractors.

Following price negotiations, Deere took an option on the purchase of the company. In a board meeting on March 14, 1918, Silloway moved that Deere buy Waterloo Gasoline Engine Company. The resolution passed unanimously and, six years after it first resolved to do so, Deere and Company entered into tractor production.

Waterloo, Iowa, home of Waterloo Gasoline Engine Company, manufacturer of the Waterloo Boy. Deere Archives

View from the furrow: Waterloo Boy Model N fitted with grousers; June 1920. Deere Archives

Pulley-side view of Model N; taken at the factory in June 1920. Deere Archives

Rear view of platform and controls of the Waterloo Boy Model N. Deere Archives

Chapter 3

Advancement of the General-Purpose Tractor

Between 1840 and 1920, the US population swelled from 17 to more than 105 million. America was a nation burgeoning with immigrants. In 1840, 3,720,000 of its citizens were employed in agriculture—77 percent of all workers. By 1870, the percentage fell to 47 percent; by 1900, it was 35 percent; and in 1920 the percentage of farm workers stood at 26 percent, or 10 percent of the total population.

Throughout this span of eighty years, America's farmers adeptly grew the crops and raised the livestock that fed the country. How did American farmers manage to feed an exploding population, yet employ an ever-decreasing percentage of its workers? Simply put, through mechanization.

According to the US Department of Agriculture, in 1830 it required 57.7 work hours to produce one acre (twenty bushels) of wheat. The advent of the stalk cutter, walking plow, harrow, one-row planter, double-sweep cultivator, binder, thresher, and steam traction engine reduced the number to 8.8 work hours by 1896.

The amount of labor required to raise corn and cotton, America's principal row-crops, was also reduced: in 1855, it required 33.6 work hours to raise one acre (forty bushels) of corn. By 1894, following the introduction of the two-bottom gang plow, disk harrow, two-row planter, and one-row cultivator, the required labor was cut in half to 15.1 hours. In 1841 it took 140.6 work hours to produce one acre of cotton (750lb of seed cotton). By 1895, with the added help of a stalk cutter, walking plow, smoothing harrow, one-row planter, and double-sweep cultivator, labor was reduced to 96.2 hours.

Tractor Versus Horse

While agriculture's dependence on manual labor declined, its demand for horsepower esca-

The horse continued as a major source of farm power, well beyond the 1920s. In this photo, taken about 1924, wagons built by the Moline Wagon Company are pulled by a team of horses. Deere Archives

Estimated Number of Draft Animals on US Farms 1850–1920

Year	Horses	Mules	Oxen
1850	4,357,000	559,000	1,701,000
1860	6,249,000	1,151,000	2,255,000
1870	7,145,000	1,125,000	1,319,000
1880	10,357,000	1,813,000	994,000
1890	15,266,000	2,252,000	1,117,000
1900	15,506,000	2,755,000	960,000
1910	17,430,000	3,787,000	640,000
1920	17,221,000	4,652,000	370,000

Source: US Census Bureau.

lated at a striking rate. Prior to 1920, the call for more horsepower was largely answered by an increased number of draft animals.

By 1920, gas tractors as well as steam and gasoline engines supplied 30 percent of available horsepower units, while draft animals remained the source of nearly 60 percent. The horse endured, despite the fact that the tractor not only increased the rate at which field work was done, but also greatly reduced the cost of power and labor for such operations.

In the 1910s and 1920s, numerous studies were published in popular farm journals and agricultural bulletins supporting the claims of the tractor's efficiency.

In its publication *Muscles or Motors?*, International Harvester cited a study performed by the Canadian Department of Agriculture in 1926 which claimed, "in Eastern Canada and British

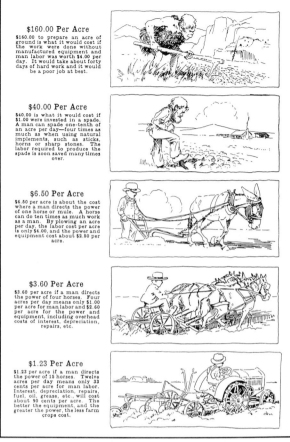

In a 1925 publication titled Muscles or Motors?, *International Harvester compared the costs of farming with and without tractor power.* Shields Library, Special Collections, University of California, Davis

John Deere's Low Down spreader pulled by a team of horses, circa 1920. Deere Archives

Columbia the two-plough tractor not only ploughs more than three times as much per day as the two-horse team but does this at one-half the cost per acre."

A study conducted at North Dakota State College of Agriculture focused on the amount of time a farmer spent on the care of horses. The report, published in Bulletin No. 165, concluded that "the average amount of time required to take care of the work horses was 88 hours per year per horse."

The farmer who operated a 200 acre corn-belt farm in the 1920s might well have maintained a stable of ten horses. At eighty-eight hours per horse per year, the study suggested that the farmer spent the equivalent of three and one-half months of eight-hour days caring for his horses.

If these reports were not disheartening enough, another study concluded that draft horses consumed, as feed, nearly one-fourth of a farm's crop production.

Ploughing Costs Per Acre (1926)

Implement	Cost per acre
Two-horse team	$3.33
Three-horse team	3.00
Four-horse team	2.33
Two-plough tractor	1.65
Three-plough tractor	1.52

Source: *Muscles or Motors?*, published by International Harvester Company

Row-Crops Dominate Agriculture

Despite the fact that the tractor was the most practical source of power for plowing, in 1925 fewer than one farm in eight employed tractors.

Without question, widespread acceptance of tractors was hampered by the fact that they were expensive to purchase. Yet, there is an even more practical explanation for the limited success of the early tractor.

Universal Motor Cultivator, on display at the Smithsonian Institution in Washington, D.C. The Universal was the most successful of the motorized cultivators that preceded the row-crop tractor. Smithsonian Institution

In 1920, the USDA reported that 59 percent of the field crops raised in the United States required both plowing and cultivating. Moreover, it was estimated that 75 percent of all US farms raised some crop that required cultivation.

As long as the tractor could not operate as a source of power to plant and cultivate row-crops, the majority of farmers had no choice but to maintain an adequate stable of draft animals. And, if a farmer had to maintain horses or mules to plant and cultivate his row-crops, why not use the animals to plow as well? Why purchase a tractor and duplicate a source of horsepower? In 1920, the tractor was still an extravagance that most farmers simply could not justify.

Motor Cultivator Leads To General-Purpose Tractor

The call for a "universal" tractor, one that could serve as a source of power in all field and stationary applications, came early in the history of the gasoline tractor. By 1910, articles regularly appeared in engineering and popular farm journals calling for its development. While the Farmall did not appear before 1923, motor cultivators, the earliest strides toward a row-crop tractor, first appeared about 1914.

The Universal Motor Cultivator was among the first and most successful of its type. Introduced by the Universal Tractor Manufacturing Company in 1915, its production was soon taken over by Moline Plow Company (which in 1929 merged with Minneapolis Steel and Machinery Company to become Minneapolis-Moline).

In its earliest days, the Universal Motor Cultivator was powered by a two-cylinder, 10hp Reliable engine. By 1918, it was transformed into a lightweight, four-cylinder tractor equipped with electric start, and to which, according to C. H. Wendel, "with slight modifications, almost any farm implement could be adapted. . . ."

Between 1915 and 1920, several other companies introduced motorized equipment designed exclusively for cultivating. Among them were machines built by International Harvester, Toro, Allis-Chalmers, Parrett, Avery, Emerson-Brantingham, and Taylor. While both the Universal and the more specialized motor cultivators achieved a degree of success, they ultimately failed as tractors. Most were underpowered and none offered a belt pulley.

As Wayne Broehl wrote, "What was needed was not more specialized equipment with minimal versatility, but less specialized equipment with maximum versatility."

The Marseilles plant built twenty-five examples of the one-row Tractivator. According to historian Don Mac- *millan, Deere's efforts at building a motorized cultivator fell victim to the 1920–1921 depression.* Deere Archives

*International Harvester motor cultivator. Note large
wheels in front, with narrow wheels trailing; 1916.* State
Historical Society of Wisconsin

*By 1921, International Harvester had turned running
gear around with narrow wheels in front and mounted*
engine parallel to frame. Note the steering mechanism.
State Historical Society of Wisconsin

Automotive Industries, journal of the Society of Automotive Engineers (SAE), and *Agricultural Engineering,* journal of the American Society of Agricultural Engineers (ASAE) are fertile sources of information regarding the development of the general-purpose tractor. From the late 1910s through the 1930s, numerous articles appeared that chronicled its advancement.

In March 1919, *Automotive Industries* wrote, "It is generally realized that before the farmer can dispense with his horses he must be offered machines for doing all the different kinds of work for which he now uses horses." The author called for "specially light tractors with high clearance, to which cultivators similar to the horse-drawn implements [could] be hitched."

In the February 1920 issue of *Agricultural Engineering,* William C. Zelle, president of Zelle Tractor Company, reviewed features that he considered desirable in a general farm tractor. Those features included a horsepower requirement of 8 to 16hp; ability to perform a wide range of work; ample clearance, light ground pressure, and a wheel gauge that would enable the tractor to run through rows without injuring the crop; short turning radius; ability to straddle one row while cultivating two rows; a four-forward-speed transmission, providing for a "trouble speed" of 1mph, plowing speed of 2.33mph, a cultivating speed of 3.75mph, and a road speed of 5mph; power lift, for raising attachments by means of engine power; PTO; fully enclosed gearing; and a generally foolproof design.

In a May 1924 article that appeared in *Agricultural Engineering,* F. A. Wirt, manager of sales promotion for J. I. Case Threshing Machine Company, called for a general-purpose tractor that "should pull a [14in] two-bottom plow . . . operate a [20] or [22in] thresher, and with the proper attachment cultivate two rows at a time."

Zelle and Wirt's insightful suggestions were representative of many of the features that were

Later prototype with fuel tank in front of engine; April 1922. State Historical Society of Wisconsin

incorporated into general-purpose tractor designs produced by International Harvester and Deere and Company.

The Farmall

A study of International Harvester's archival photographs clearly reveals that the Farmall evolved directly from the successful IHC motor cultivator introduced in 1916.

Developed over a period of five years, the Farmall's distinctive features included a high-clearance rear axle (30in above the ground), which allowed it to drive over young corn and cotton plants; 74in rear wheel tread, which permitted it to straddle two rows; narrow front wheels, which could run between two rows; and a series of matching implements, which permitted the Farmall to cultivate two rows at a time and plant either two or four rows at a time. In addition, the Farmall offered PTO and a belt pulley. Still, the Farmall was sold in limited quantities prior to 1928.

In January 1928, Farmall production reached sixty-five units a day; by the following June,

Farmall Production 1923–1927

Year	Production
1923	22
1924	205
1925	838
1926	4,430
1927	9,502

production was up to 125 units per day. By January 1930, it hit 200 units a day, and on April 12, 1930, the Harvester Works in Rock Island, Illinois, assembled the 100,000th Farmall.

Limited production notwithstanding, the Farmall's influence on the industry was immediate, profound, and lasting. All manufacturers reacted and initiated or accelerated development of their own "all-purpose" designs. In 1928, the Rumely Do-All and John Deere General Purpose 10-20 (GP) were the first to follow.

By 1930, the Massey-Harris Company had introduced its General Purpose model, a four-

This prototype of July 1922 featured high frame, pedestal-mounted steering gear, and sheet metal closely resem- bling the Farmall production unit. State Historical Society of Wisconsin

Preproduction Farmall unit of February 1923. State
Historical Society of Wisconsin

*Preproduction Farmall with integral cultivator; April
1923.* State Historical Society of Wisconsin

Early production Farmall, photographed at the factory.
State Historical Society of Wisconsin

wheel-drive row-crop tractor. Oliver Farm Equipment Company, created in 1929 from the merger of Oliver Chilled Plow Works, Hart-Parr Company, American Seeding Machinery, and the venerable Nichols and Shepard Company, introduced its model the Oliver Hart-Parr Row Crop. J. I. Case Company, no longer the J. I. Case Threshing Machine Company, debuted the Model CC. And Minneapolis-Moline, formed in 1929, premiered the Twin City KT (Kombination Tractor).

In 1931, Allis-Chalmers entered the field with the Model UC All-Crop; Huber developed the Modern Farmer; the Graham-Bradley GP made its first appearance in the Sears Roebuck mail-order catalog; and significantly, International Harvester introduced the Farmall F-30, a larger brother to its original model now referred to as the Regular.

Impact Of The General-Purpose Tractor

Between 1925 and 1930 the number of tractors on US farms increased by 80 percent, from 505,933 to over 920,000. Sales of general-purpose tractors proved strong, as farmers welcomed the economy and versatility these tractors offered. By 1940,

general-purpose tractors comprised 90 percent of the 249,397 wheel tractors manufactured in the United States.

Able to plow, plant, cultivate, and harvest any type of crop, the general-purpose tractor significantly reduced the work hours needed to produce row-crops. With the added benefits of the general-purpose tractor an acre of corn, which in 1896 required 15.1 hours to produce, required only 6.9 work hours in 1930.

As general-purpose tractors, disk plows, and two-row middlebusters and cultivators moved onto Southern cotton farms an acre of cotton, which in 1895 required 96.2 work hours to produce, required 71.8 hours of labor by 1930.

As more farmers adopted tractors, the demand for draft animals plunged. By 1930, draft animals supplied less than 25 percent of the available horsepower on US farms. By 1950, when approximately 500,000 wheel tractors were sold, fewer than 7 million horses remained on American farms. No longer needed to walk between the rows, Ol' Dobbin was finally let out to pasture.

Chapter 4

John Deere Models C and GP

The General Purpose Model 10-20, or Model GP, was Deere and Company's first successful effort at a row-crop tractor. Introduced in 1927 as the Model C, it was modified and reintroduced the following year as the Model GP. Full-scale production began at the Waterloo tractor plant in March 1928 and continued into April 1935.

While maligned by some for its three-row configuration and a shortage of horsepower, the GP's innovative mechanical power lift and matched integral implements set an industry standard. Despite its drawbacks, more than 35,000 Model

GPs were built during its eight-year production run.

The Men Behind Deere's First GP Tractor

In 1925, Charles Deere Wiman, then Deere and Company's director of manufacturing, charged Theo Brown with the responsibility of developing an "all-crop" tractor.

Wiman's commitment to the All-Crop was a bold move. Since 1921, Deere had suffered significant losses in its tractor operations. Moreover, about the same time that he ordered work to begin on the new tractor, Wiman also committed Deere to further development and manufacture of both a combine and a corn picker.

Three critical experimental programs such as these demanded substantial commitments of capital and personnel. Yet, Wiman understood that without a vigorous product development program, Deere would not be prepared to meet the competition posed by International Harvester, Case, and

Charles Deere Wiman, company president from 1928 to 1955. An innovative and highly respected leader, Wiman directed the company through the Depression, World War II, and the postwar boom. Deere Archives

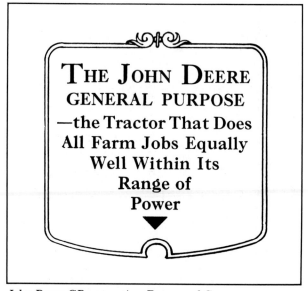

THE JOHN DEERE
GENERAL PURPOSE
—the Tractor That Does
All Farm Jobs Equally
Well Within Its
Range of
Power
▼

John Deere GP promotion. Deere and Co.

the other full-line manufacturers that had emerged in the 1910s and 1920s.

Theo Brown was well qualified for the assignment. A 1901 graduate of the Worcester (Massachusetts) Polytechnic Institute, Brown began his career with the Richardson Manufacturing Company, where he designed the Beater-on-the-Axle manure spreader.

In 1911, Brown joined the Marseilles Company as plant superintendent. By 1916, he had moved to the manager's position in the Experimental Department at Deere and Company. As such, he was involved in many of the company's early tractor and motor cultivator experiments.

Three-Row Cultivator

Wayne G. Broehl, Jr., stated that right from the start, Brown decided the All-Crop should be configured in such a way that it would be able to handle a three-row cultivator.

In retrospect, this decision is generally viewed as having been a mistake. In 1925, one-, two-, and occasionally four-row operations were common. However, the notion of cultivating three rows was outside conventional practice.

Add to the three-row notion the prospect of doing the work with a tractor—a source of power alien to most farmers—and it is not difficult to appreciate the disadvantage at which Deere placed itself. Once introduced, acceptance of the All-Crop tractor's three-row design was further thwarted by the tractor's relative lack of horsepower.

The two-cylinder engine fitted to the All-Crop was short on reserve horsepower. Under normal field conditions, it offered adequate power to cultivate three rows or pull a 14in two-bottom plow. Yet, on hillsides or under heavy soil conditions, the tractor's performance paled in comparison to that of the Farmall. (Note: In the official Nebraska tests, the Farmall's drawbar pull under maximum load was rated at 2,727lb at 12.7hp, whereas the drawbar pull of the GP was rated at 2,489lb at 17.24hp.)

Introduction of the Model C

Work on the All-Crop began in 1925. Three prototypes were built by July 1926, and field tests were conducted throughout the summer of 1927 (Don Macmillan and Russell Jones reported a total of five prototypes). Beginning in March 1927 and ending in January 1928, about 110 tractors were built and designated Model C.

The new tractor's weaknesses were recognized early in its development. Yet, by the time thorough field tests were completed, Wiman felt that the company could not defer full-scale production of the tractor.

One reason was the success of IHC's Models 15-30 and 10-20, which had restored the manufacturer to its position as leader in tractor sales by 1927. Fordson had been rebuffed, and the further excitement and anticipation generated by the Farmall—even though fewer than 5,500 units had been built through 1926—also had propelled IHC to the fore.

In addition to the challenges presented by International Harvester, Wiman was under pres-

Theo Brown; taken December 1936. Deere Archives

The Model C was the forerunner of the Model GP, Deere's first row-crop tractor. Few survived in their original state. This Model C belongs to the Keller family of Forest Junction, Wisconsin.

Frank Silloway was a Deere board member who, along with George Peek, was largely responsible for the company's marketing successes during the 1920s and 1930s. Deere Archives

sure from Deere's field personnel and dealers, who clamored for the new tractor. Ultimately, a commitment was made to expand the tractor plant to accommodate assembly of the new tractor. Soon, full-scale production was begun of the first Deere general-purpose tractor.

Years later, Deere president Wiman referred to this first general-purpose tractor as an "outstanding failure." He stated, "Well do I recall how much tractor business was lost by our company due to bad design of the 'GP' line."

All-Crop Becomes the General Purpose

According to Broehl, Deere and Company general sales manager Frank Silloway was responsible for naming the new tractor. He first considered two suggestions: Powerfarmer and Farmrite.

Silloway rejected those names, however; he was concerned that either choice would detract from the Model D, the successor to the Waterloo Boy and the model he considered to be Deere's "real power farmer tractor."

Silloway declared, "We do not care to popularize with a name such as 'Powerfarmer,' the smaller tractor on which we make little profit, as against the Model D which is a profitable tractor for both the dealer and ourselves to sell and the one that most farmers should buy."

As stated, the new tractor was first designated the Model C. However, when dealers placed orders by telephone, the similarity in sound between the designations Model C and Model D sometimes

The Model C, forerunner of the Model GP, cultivating corn; June 1928. Deere Archives

resulted in confusion. Silloway cited this reason when he opted for the initials GP. From then on, the term general-purpose replaced all-crop in Deere lexicon.

Overview of the Model GP

The Model GP was built in five distinct versions through the course of its production:

• The standard-front GP, or Standard, built from March 1928 to February 1935

• The two-wheel tricycle-front GP, or GP-Tricycle, of which twenty-three units were built between August 1928 and April 1929

• The GP Wide-Tread, or GPWT, built from November 1929 to November 1933

• The GP Wide-Tread Series P, a GPWT with narrowed rear tread width designed to suit potato rows, built between January and August 1930

• The General Purpose Orchard tractor, or GPO, built from April 1931 to April 1935.

Deere's Two-Cylinder Engine

As with all Deere tractors built prior to 1961, the GP's two-cylinder engine was one of its most distinctive features.

Deere built well over one million two-cylinder engines in a period of more than forty years. Celebrated for its distinctive popping noise, once described as sounding like "an angry motorboat,"

Cutaway of a Waterloo Boy two-cylinder engine. Deere's exclusive commitment to two-cylinders persisted for more than four decades. Deere Archives

Flywheel-side view of an early GP. Note the elliptical-shaped exhaust and standard twenty-four-lug rear wheels; December 1929. Deere Archives

Model GP horizontal, valve-in-block, two-cylinder engine.

the Deere two-cylinder engine earned a reputation as a reliable, economical, and easy-to-service engine.

Deere's choice of the two-cylinder engine was largely dictated by cost. In 1922, Leon Clausen, who preceded Wiman as director of manufacturing, sought board approval to develop a four-cylinder

engine for use in what became the Model D. However, because sales of the Waterloo Boy tractor were so poor in 1921 (seventy-nine units sold) and 1922 (with losses exceeding $400,000), the company held a large inventory of two-cylinder engines. The board rejected Clausen's request for a four-cylinder engine on the basis that the company was not in a position to spend the money. Clausen had no choice but to make use of the existing engine inventory.

As Broehl stated in *John Deere's Company*, the board made the decision to continue with the two-cylinder engine "not on technical grounds but on the basis of [a] short-term embarrassed financial situation."

How ironic that the two-cylinder engine, almost abandoned in 1922, survived to become so closely associated with John Deere tractors and their success.

The engine used in all versions of the Model GP, including the Model C, was easily distinguished from that fitted to any other model of Deere tractor. It was the only valve-in-block, flat-head engine built by the company. A horizontal design, the engine was mounted crosswise on the frame, with its flywheel on the left-hand side of the tractor.

Model GP with integral four-row cultivator; October 1929. Deere Archives

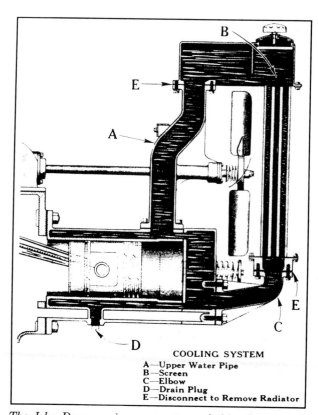

COOLING SYSTEM
A—Upper Water Pipe
B—Screen
C—Elbow
D—Drain Plug
E—Disconnect to Remove Radiator

The John Deere engine was water-cooled by the thermo-siphoning system, using a straight-tube radiator core and positive shaft-driven fan. No belts or water pump were required. Deere and Co.

At introduction, the GP's engine featured a 5³/₄x6in bore and stroke. Lubricated by a gear-driven oil pump, it was cooled by of gear-driven fan and thermosiphon circulation system.

Engine spark was generated by a Fairbanks-Morse magneto. The carburetor was a double-nozzle type, with air choke. The engine was fitted with a Donaldson-Simplex oil-soaked, fiber-filament air cleaner that was contained in a canister positioned between the top of the engine and the fan.

In 1929, an air intake stack with optional auxiliary air cleaner was fitted to the right-hand side of the engine, and in 1930 an exhaust stack was fitted to the left-hand side.

Kerosene and Distillates

Kerosene and distillates, both byproducts that were created when oil was distilled to produce gasoline, were cheaper than gasoline and commonly used fuel sources well into the 1940s. Heavier than gasoline, kerosene and distillates were also less flammable. As such, they required higher temperatures to ignite and burn efficiently.

To permit efficient use of kerosene, distillates, furnace oil, and light grades of fuel oil, the Model GP was designed to start and warm up on gasoline. When engine temperature hit a range of 180 to 190 degrees Fahrenheit, the operator manually switched the fuel supply to the lower grade fuel. To permit use of both fuels, the tractor was fitted with dual fuel tanks.

Preignition was a common problem when low grades of fuel were used. Consequently, the GP was fitted with a water valve through which the flow of water into the combustion chamber was controlled, and preignition was dampened.

More than a row-crop tractor, the GP pulls a Beater-on-the-Axle type spreader; November 1929. Deere Archives

Engine Rating

The General Purpose was fitted with a "fly-ball" type governor that was set to maintain engine speed of 950rpm under load and 1000rpm at idle.

As stated, the GP suffered from a lack of horsepower. Wiman had "hoped that the tractor would develop at least 25 hp in order to give proper feel of performance. . . ." It did not, however.

Running under "rated load" in its Nebraska test of October 22–29, 1928 (Official Tractor Test No. 153), the GP's engine generated 20.20hp at the belt pulley and 10.20hp at the drawbar. Improved performance followed in 1931, when a larger-bore engine was introduced.

Model GP with spike-toothed harrow; December 1929. Deere Archives

Early Model GP with two-row Lister; December 1929. Deere Archives

Specialized equipment, such as this bean harvester, added to the versatility of the Standard GP; July 1931. Deere Archives

Model GP with modified manifold and exhaust, and trailing Van Brunt cultivator; June 1930. Deere Archives

Steering, Transmission, Clutch, and Final Drives

The GP was fitted with automotive-type worm-gear steering, with a drag link that ran at the right-hand side of the tractor. The transmission featured three speeds forward and one reverse speed: low, 2⅓mph; intermediate, 3⅛mph; high, 4⅓mph; and reverse, 2mph.

The tractor was fitted with a hand clutch controlled by a lever to the right of the operator. Power was transferred from the differential to the final drives by roller chain. Differential brakes to each drive wheel ensured a tight, 8ft turning radius.

Model GP Standard-Front Performance

Deere promoted the GP as "A Standard Outfit That [Did] All Farm Work," and declared it the first tractor to employ four methods of farm power: drawbar, belt pulley, power takeoff, and mechanical power lift.

The Standard was the original version of the GP. Its arched front axle clearance was 24in at center. Platform clearance was 22in, and the rear wheel tread width was 49½in, center to center. The standard front wheels were 24x6in "dust-proof" type. The rear wheels were 42¾x10in forged-steel rims with twenty-four 4in spade lugs. This configuration permitted the GP to straddle one row and, with its purpose-built, integral (mounted) cultivator, cultivate three rows at a time.

A Model GP with optional AC-560 air cleaner with Vertical Auxiliary Cleaner powers a No. 5 combine; August 1930. Deere Archives

According to Deere sales literature, "With the John Deere General Purpose Tractor and Three-Row Cultivator, one man [could] cultivate thoroughly, from 25 to 40 acres per day, depending upon the height of the corn and field conditions. Translated into terms of one-row, horse-drawn equipment, this outfit [would] do as much work as, or even more than four men and eight horses. . . ."

The GP was rated as a "two-plow tractor," able to pull two 14in bottoms. It was particularly well suited to the Model 40C plow. Developed by Deere

Model GP with power binder featured here with a remote steering system and unusual exhaust stack to carry exhaust above and away from operator; August 1930. Deere Archives

GP tractor with rotary hoe. Intake stack on pulley side and exhaust stack on opposite side indicate this unit was fitted with the 6x6in engine; May 1931. Deere Archives

Standard GP with plow. Exhaust is on right-hand side, intake on left-hand side; November 1930. Deere Archives

for the Fordson, the Model 40C Tractor Plow was "especially designed for plowing conditions that [were] not extreme."

With its standard-front end, the GP's front and rear wheels remained in the furrow during plowing. Deere promoted this, as well as the straight center hitch for both plow and tractor, as "eliminating side draft."

An integral planter, the GP301 was developed for use with the GP. According to Deere, the three-row unit operated with "the accuracy for which John Deere No. 999 Planters [were] famous." With it, one farmer could "plant from 30 to 40 acres per day . . . [and] do the work of two to three men with horse-drawn two-row planters."

In addition to the mounted three-row planter and cultivator, Deere developed an integral sweep rake and a PTO-powered sicklebar mower for the GP.

Belt Pulley

The belt pulley was a feature available on all farm tractors. It was, of course, one of the earliest

Studio artwork depicts pulley-side view of early Model GP. The rear steel wheels are standard 4in spade lugs.

Optional 5in spade lugs were available, for use in loose top soil. Deere Archives

The GP provided four sources of power, including the belt power to drive this baler. Deere Archives

means by which mechanical power was applied to farm work.

In the 1920s, there were no industry standards for belt pulley size or speed. The Model GP featured a 13in diameter pulley 6½in wide that was driven directly off the crankshaft. It ran at 950rpm—the same speed as the engine—or a belt speed of 3,200 feet per minute (fpm).

Power was transferred to the pulley through a friction clutch that was engaged by the clutch lever located to the right of the operator.

Power Takeoff

The GP's optional engine-driven PTO offered the third mode of tractor power. Mounted to the flywheel side of the tractor and engaged by means of a separate gear shift, the AC-380 Power Shaft offered front and rear 1⅛in splined shafts that rotated clockwise at 520rpm.

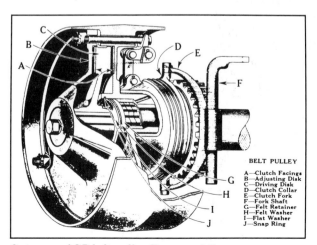

BELT PULLEY

A—Clutch Facings
B—Adjusting Disk
C—Driving Disk
D—Clutch Collar
E—Clutch Fork
F—Fork Shaft
G—Felt Retainer
H—Felt Washer
I—Flat Washer
J—Snap Ring

Cutaway of GP belt pulley. Deere and Co.

The AC-521 (Mechanical) Power-Lift Attachment mounted beneath the AC-380 Power Shaft.

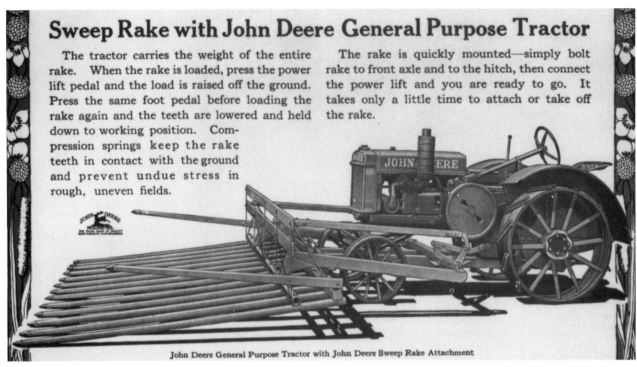

Sweep Rake with John Deere General Purpose Tractor

The tractor carries the weight of the entire rake. When the rake is loaded, press the power lift pedal and the load is raised off the ground. Press the same foot pedal before loading the rake again and the teeth are lowered and held down to working position. Compression springs keep the rake teeth in contact with the ground and prevent undue stress in rough, uneven fields.

The rake is quickly mounted—simply bolt rake to front axle and to the hitch, then connect the power lift and you are ready to go. It takes only a little time to attach or take off the rake.

John Deere General Purpose Tractor with John Deere Sweep Rake Attachment

Deere sales literature advertised the benefits of power-lift rake and tractor. Note the optional spark-arresting muffler. Deere Archives

Business Week *magazine reported that only 5 percent of tractors sold in 1933 came equipped with rubber. By 1935, it was up to 45 percent. This Model GP has factory-* equipped *Firestone turf-tires; December 1933.* Deere Archives

Mechanical Power Lift

The mechanical power lift was the most innovative feature of the Model GP. It was touted as the "fourth form" of tractor power. Driven by the engine, it provided a mechanical means by which attachments could be raised and lowered, with the "touch of a foot" to a pedal linked to the rear of the device.

An optional feature, the AC-521 Power Lift Attachment, had to be ordered along with the AC-380 Power Shaft, to which it was mounted and through which engine power was transferred.

Devised by Theo Brown and his engineering group, the mechanical power lift soon became a feature available on most general-purpose tractors.

Special Equipment

In addition to the power takeoff and mechanical power lift, a variety of optional equipment was offered for the GP. Included were a number of wheel options, lighting equipment, and fenders. Three pages of Special Equipment, reproduced from the booklet titled John Deere General Purpose Two-Cylinder Tractor, appear at the end of this section.

Standard Model GP with "bean" front axle. Deere Archives

Standard GP Modified

In 1931, the Standard GP was modified and a larger engine was introduced. Beginning with tractor serial number 223,803, engine bore was increased by 1/2in.

Fitted with rubber tires, Deere offered this adapted GP for "industrial service such as inter-plant transportation, and hauling on paved streets and roads." The tractor featured 40x8in rear wheels and 24in front wheels with either 3½ or 5in face. According to sales literature, "an expanding wedge device in the steel wheel rim [made] possible the removal and replacement of rubber tires without the use of a wheel press." The GP could be fitted with special sprockets and drive chains to provide a range of higher speed, which "[fitted] the tractor to the work required and [secured] the most in capacity and efficiency." (December 1930) Deere Archives

Note wider front tread and tie-rod placement behind the axle; February 1931. Deere Archives

Exhaust with spark-arresting muffler on pulley side; intake with vertical auxiliary air cleaner on flywheel side. A series of factory photos of the "New" Standard

Model GP, with 6x6in engine; November 1930. Deere Archives

The result was a significant boost in horse-power. In its Nebraska test of May 4–15, 1931 (Official Tractor Test No. 190), running under rated load the GP's new 6x6in engine generated 24.14hp at the belt pulley and 15.34hp at the drawbar.

With the change in engine came other modifications, including a change in exhaust from the flywheel side to the pulley side. (Refer to the specifications and Nebraska test results in this section for more details.)

GP-Tricycle

Although a few Model C units were built with a tricycle front end, the original version of the Model GP was available with a standard front only. The introduction of a two-wheel tricycle front soon followed. Production of fifty GP-Tricycles was allocated. However, only twenty-three units were manufactured, between August 18, 1928, and April 15, 1929.

Two to six GP-Tricycles were built with 68in rear tread width, for use in potato rows. Three of

Of twenty-three Model GP Tricycles built, only one tractor is known to have survived. Its owners are the Keller family.

Model GP Tricycle viewed head-on.

these units were shipped to Maine. The remaining seventeen to twenty-one units were essentially the Standard GP, but with a tricycle front. Most of these units were shipped to Texas, presumably for sale to cotton growers, who had largely rejected the Standard version's wide front end.

Production of the GP-Tricycle was suspended, following introduction of the General Purpose Wide-Tread. Prized by collectors, only one example of the GP-Tricycle is known to exist.

General Purpose Wide-Tread

The Standard GP with its three-row design was better accepted in the North than in the South, where cotton growers preferred the tricycle-front, wide-tread rear axle, and two- or four-row configuration of the Farmall.

Farmers complained that the GP's broad hood and radiator, and its standard front axle hampered their forward visibility when cultivating. (Poor visibility alone may have made the GP's three-row cultivator impractical.)

Whatever the reasons for its poor sales, Deere realized that the GP would have to be redesigned to compete with the Farmall. By November 12, 1928, Deere began manufacture of the General Purpose Wide-Tread (GPWT). The new tractor was widely available by the 1929 spring planting season.

With its two-wheel tricycle-front, wide-tread rear axle, and two- and four-row cultivators, the Wide-Tread more closely resembled the Farmall.

The General Purpose Wide-Tread was introduced with the same 5³/₄x6in engine used in the Standard model. In January 1931, the larger 6x6in bore and stroke engine was introduced in both versions.

GPWT Side and Overhead Steering

The Wide-Tread underwent several modifications through its course of production. The changes to its steering mechanism were the most radical.

The original steering system, which was offset to the right of the tractor, employed a shaft and worm that ran from the steering wheel to the

Preproduction GP Wide-Tread (GPWT) model. Featured "Southern" open steel wheels; September 1928. Deere Archives

The Model GPWT with overhead steering went into production in February 1932. Shown here as preproduc-tion unit. Fitted with Potato-style rear wheels; July 1931. Deere Archives

Early GPWT with Model 443 cultivator; February 1930. Deere Archives

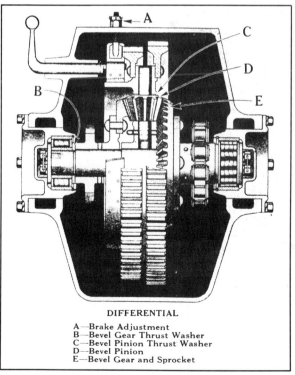

DIFFERENTIAL
A—Brake Adjustment
B—Bevel Gear Thrust Washer
C—Bevel Pinion Thrust Washer
D—Bevel Pinion
E—Bevel Gear and Sprocket

Roller chain was used to transfer power from the differential to the final drives. Deere and Co.

worm-gear housing mounted at the top and right-hand side of the transmission case.

A link dropped from the worm gear and was connected by a ball joint to the drag link that ran at the right-hand (pulley) side of the tractor, level with its frame. The drag link was connected to a steering arm, which in turn steered the yoke and spindle.

This system, referred to as side steer, is differentiated from the overhead steering system that was fitted to the Wide-Tread beginning with serial number 404,810, in February 1932.

The overhead steering system, which was set in the center of the tractor, employed a shaft and worm that ran from the steering wheel, through a support mount, and over the hood of the tractor to a bolster or pedestal mounted in front of the radiator. The worm-gear housing was mounted to the top of the bolster, with its gearing connected directly to the yoke and spindle.

The overhead steering system eliminated the front-wheel "whip" that was sometimes a problem with the less direct side-steer system.

GPWT Transmission and Final Drives

The three-speed transmission used in the Wide-Tread was rated at slightly slower speeds than that of the Standard GP. The difference was most likely due to the greater weight of the Wide-Tread. As with the Standard GP, power was transferred from the differential to the final drives by roller chain.

GPWT Design and Equipment

Deere promoted the Wide-Tread as a tractor "built for the South." In fact, the tractor was well received throughout the country.

Its design and equipment differed greatly from that of the Standard version. At 117½in overall length and 85½in overall width, the Wide-Tread was 5½in longer and 26½in wider than the Standard GP. Its wheelbase of 78⁵⁄₁₆in was nearly 8in longer than that of the Standard version.

The Wide-Tread's two-wheel tricycle front ran between two rows. Its rear wheel tread width of 76in, center to center, permitted its rear end to straddle two rows in the same manner as the Farmall.

Factory photo of Model 10 two-row cotton harvester mounted on a GP Wide-Tread; October 1929. Deere Archives

GPWT with Model 443 cultivator; February 1930. Deere
Archives

GPWT with sidesteer and crossover manifold.

Reversible 27in front wheels were standard,
with 43½x10in twenty-four-lug forged-steel rims
at the rear.

GPWT Two- and Four-Row Implements

Deere introduced a new series of two- and four-
row implements for use with the Wide-Tread.

The Deere GP400 Four-Row Cotton and Corn
Planter permitted one farmer to "plant from 35 to
45 acres a day planting in rows 36in or 38in apart,
in furrows or in beds."

Connected to the mechanical power lift, the
planter beams and furrow openers raised and
lowered by a "mere touch of the foot," while the

GP Wide-Tread with Model 400 C & C planter. Deere
Archives

planting mechanism automatically shut off when the beams were raised. The integral mounting mechanism employed heavy coil springs, which permitted the outfit to be operated on rough land without "fear of breakage."

Deere introduced a two-row bedding attachment for the GP400 planter, to which either regular middlebreaker bottoms or plow sweeps could be mounted.

A two-row Lister attachment, adjustable for listing rows 36 or 38in apart, was now offered.

The GP200 Two-Row Lister and Planter was also available for the Wide-Tread. Interchangeable plates permitted the unit to plant "any kind of corn . . . shelled peanuts [sorghum], milo maize, broom corn and . . . beans and peas." It also featured the "famous John Deere Saw-Tooth Type Steel Picker Wheel for planting cotton."

Both two- and four-row integral cultivators, Models GP202 and GP402, respectively, were introduced for the Wide-Tread. The GP202 was adjustable for rows spaced 36, 38, 40, and 42in apart while the four-row unit was adjustable for rows planted 36 or 38in apart.

GPWT Modifications

In addition to the change in steering and the introduction of the 6x6in engine, the GP Wide-Tread underwent a number of other modifications through its five-year production run.

Several changes were made to the model's air intake and exhaust systems. As with the early Standard GP, the Wide-Tread's air intake and exhaust were originally positioned underneath the tractor's hood, with the air intake on the pulley side and the exhaust on the flywheel side.

Studio photo of early GPWT with overhead steering, from flywheel side. Two holes in frame allowed for mounting integral implements. Narrow front and wider rear tread *width made the GPWT model more competitive with the Farmall; December 1931.* Deere Archives

In 1930, an air intake stack was introduced. Mounted through the hood on the pulley side of the tractor, it reduced the amount of dirt and dust drawn into the engine. An exhaust stack, which carried exhaust away from the operator and discharged sparks up and away from potentially dry grass or stubble, also appeared in 1930.

In late 1930, the air intake was modified and its stack was placed outside the hood. A special crossover exhaust manifold was bolted to the flywheel (left-hand) side of the engine. It crossed in front of the engine to the pulley (right-hand) side. With this arrangement, both the intake and exhaust were positioned on the pulley side of the tractor.

The crossover manifold was carried over to the 6x6in engine, which was adopted at serial number 402,040. However, in early 1931, at serial number 402,445, the crossover manifold was eliminated. In its place was a new exhaust manifold that crossed above the engine to exit on the pulley side, with its exhaust stack outside the hood. A spark-arresting muffler was incorporated into the exhaust, and the intake stack was then fitted to the pulley side of the engine.

Other options and changes are worthy of note as well. In 1931, a seat was offered that swung from side to side and permitted the operator to gain a better view of row-crop work. In 1932, in an effort to improve forward visibility the Wide-Tread's hood was narrowed and tapered, and to improve operator comfort the standard tractor seat was mounted on an adjustable cushion spring in later models.

The last General Purpose Wide-Tread was built in November 1933. While the Wide-Tread did not displace the Farmall from its dominant position, it was a more credible challenger. Many of its features were carried over to its successor, the Model A.

Model GP Series P: Potato Growers' Special

As stated earlier, of the twenty-three General Purpose Tricycles built, at least two—and perhaps as many as six—featured the 68in rear tread width suited for use in potato rows.

Introduced in 1930 for potato growers in Maine, the Model GPWT Series P featured 68in tread width, rather than the GPWT's 74in width. A total of 202 units were sold. Featured here with Hoover Planter, May 1931. Deere Archives

In November 1929, presumably as a result of the experience gained with these units, Deere decided to build a special "potato" tractor, designated the General Purpose Wide-Tread Series P.

As production of the GP-Tricycle had ended, the new tractor was based on the General Purpose Wide-Tread. To permit a shortened 68in wheel tread, the Wide-Tread's right and left quills were shortened and the differential shaft altered.

Prior to production of the Series P, the factory estimated annual demand at 150 units. In fact, a total of 203 units were built in two production runs before production was terminated.

The first run commenced January 30, 1930, with serial number P5000 and ended February 27 with serial number P5149. By the end of the first production run, Deere had introduced the 6x6in engine. The company was also prepared to introduce an offset rear wheel for the Wide-Tread that effectively narrowed its rear tread width to 68in. This new wheel made the Series P redundant.

According to *Two-Cylinder*, the official publication of the Two-Cylinder Club, "to keep all the 'P' tractors alike, and to satisfy existing orders prior to offering [the] special potato wheel for the regular Wide-Tread," Deere converted an existing inventory of seventy-three 5³⁄₄in bore Standard

tractors to Series P specifications. This final run of Series P tractors commenced on July 25, 1930, with serial number P5150 and ended August 19, 1930, with serial number P5202.

The Series P was fitted with power takeoff and mechanical power lift as standard equipment. Other alterations included modifications to the brake cams and drawbar. In the front were 24x4in steel wheels equipped with Standard GP front guide bands. Rear wheels were 44x8in steel, punched for either sixteen or twenty-four lugs. Optional 44x6in wheel extensions with eight lugs were offered (for details, see specification charts later in this section).

With production limited to 203 units, the General Purpose Series P remains one of the most sought after of Deere tractor models.

General Purpose Orchard Tractor

In 1929, Lindeman Power and Equipment, a Deere dealer located in Yakima, Washington, lowered the clearance height of a Standard Model GP to allow its use in orchards. Lindeman fitted a new front axle and modified the quill castings, which lowered the tractor's overall height by 7in.

Once completed, the tractor was demonstrated for Deere and Company officials. Impressed by

The GP Orchard tractor, or GPO, fitted with field fenders; March 1931. Deere Archives

Model GPO with power takeoff-driven mower. Note lowered seating position and protection offered by fenders; July 1935. Deere Archives

Pulley side of Model GPO. Note the exhaust. This example is fitted with orchard fenders; March 1931. Deere Archives

Lindeman's concept, Deere agreed to build its own prototypes incorporating features of the Lindeman design.

Deere began with six stock General Purpose Wide-Tread units (serial numbers 402,115; 402,128; 402,138; 402,147; 402,245; and 402,250) and modified them to suit. The units featured the 6x6in engine with crossover manifold.

To reduce its height, Deere engineers employed a lower front axle and reversed the rear axle housing which thereby lowered the tractor's mainframe. This ingenious modification permitted the operator platform to be dropped behind the housing, and positioned the operator between the rear wheels and fenders. Furthermore, the tractor's intake stack was eliminated and the exhaust stack and muffler were positioned horizontally and parallel to the tractor frame.

Measured at the radiator cap, the overall height of the orchard version was reduced by 8½in from that of the Wide-Tread, and by 7in from that of the Standard model.

Between July and September 1930, the six prototypes were shipped to Washington and California for evaluation. In February 1931, the company decided to proceed with manufacture of the General Purpose Orchard tractor, or GPO, and production began on April 2, 1931.

Production was forecast at 300 units for 1931 and 600 units for 1932. Approximately 725 GPOs were built between April 1931 and April 1935, before the tractor was superseded by the standard-tread Models AO and BO (Models A and B orchard versions). The GPO's limited success was most likely due to the depressed economy of the early 1930s.

The General Purpose Orchard tractor was available with a number of options and modifications, which included cast front wheels that would not catch branches; full "citrus" fenders, which kept branches away from the operator and out of the rear wheel spokes; balloon tires for use on turf; and a track machine, of which approximately twenty-five units were built by Lindeman.

General Purpose versus Farmall

The Farmall was, of course, the standard against which the Model GP was judged, and reaction to the GP was mixed at best.

While a number of early units broke down in the field, the Standard GP's reliability was less in question than were its standard front axle, its three-row configuration, and its shortage of horsepower.

The Farmall's configuration differed greatly from that of the GP. It featured a vertical, four-cylinder engine mounted parallel to the frame. At rated load it offered 18.03 belt horsepower and 9.35 drawbar horsepower.

Studio artwork depicts GPO. This model had hard rubber tires and full citrus fenders. Deere Archives

Special Equipment

John Deere General Purpose with Rubber-Tired Wheels

The addition of rubber-tired wheels to General Purpose Tractor adapts it to industrial service such as inter-plant transportation, and hauling on paved streets and roads. With its exceptionally short turning radius and ease of control, the General Purpose Tractor is ideally suited to factory hauling.

Rear wheels are 40 inches in diameter with 8-inch face; front wheels 24 inches in diameter with either 3½-inch or 5-inch face are furnished.

Extension wheels 8 inches in width are also furnished for service requiring exceptional tractive ability. Skid chains are available to meet conditions requiring their use. An expanding wedge device in the steel wheel rim makes possible the removal and replacement of rubber tires without the use of a wheel press.

Special sprockets and drive chains can be furnished to provide a range of higher speeds—fitting the tractor to the work required and securing the most in capacity and efficiency.

AD-450 5-Inch Spade Lugs

Five-inch spade lugs are supplied for work in loose top soil where deep penetration is necessary to secure traction. AD-187, four-inch spade lugs are furnished as regular equipment, and are satisfactory for the great majority of operating conditions. For best results, lug should penetrate to its full depth; the high lugs should not be used in hard soil. The six-inch spade lug cannot be used on the General Purpose Tractor.

AD-198 Extension Angle Grousers

Extension angle grousers 4 inches high and 22 inches long. Angle grousers are furnished when required. Also available 2¼ inches high and 16 inches long—AD-189.

AC-470 Meadow Lugs

Meadow lugs made of channel steel with upright legs only ⅝-inch high. Provide necessary traction in hay fields without damage to crops.

AC-449 Road Lugs

For service on finished roads, where spade lugs or angle grousers are prohibited—and where greater traction is required than is secured through use of road bands—the malleable road lug is furnished.

Traction and, of course, pulling capacity with this type of lug is considerably less than with spade lugs or angle grousers, because of lack of penetration. Used mainly for transport or hauling light loads.

AC-593-Button Lugs

For hay field use. Provide sufficient traction for ordinary conditions with minimum damage to sod.

AC-647-Cone Lugs

For use in hay fields under conditions requiring more traction than can be had with button lugs, meadow lugs or overbands. The cone shape of these lugs permits them to enter and leave the sod without tearing.

The Economical Tractor That Burns Low-Cost Fuel

Model GP Special Equipment listing.

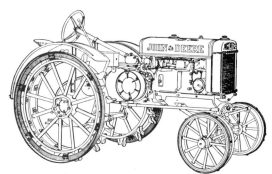

AC-403 Hay Field Overbands

Hay field overbands are attached to rear wheels and allow the spade lugs to penetrate three-fourths to an inch deep which will afford sufficient traction for the pulling of hay tools. Flat front wheel guide bands are also provided in lieu of the regular angle iron guide bands. Prevents cutting of sod and injury of cut hay.

AC-337 Road Bands

Driving tractors with spade lugs or grousers on finished roads is prohibited by law in some states. AC-337 road bands meet the requirements of state laws as to proper width. Can be easily put on or taken off. Fits over any type of lug equipment. Gives traction similar to a smooth tire. It increases the diameter of the rear wheel 10 inches, and therefore road speed materially.

AC-241 6½-Inch Extension Rims

Extension rims 6½ inches wide may be attached to the regular rear wheel with clips, as shown, when it is desired to use spade lugs, or they may be attached by extension angle grousers, AD-198. When extension angle grousers are used, clips are not required. Either one or two sets of extension rims may be used.

When extension rims are necessary in planting corn, the 4-inch wide extension rim, AC-340, can be furnished. This rim provides sufficient clearance between the planter attachment and rim.

AC-99 Front Wheel Extension Rims

Front wheel extension rim is desirable for work in swamps and very muddy land. Attached to the regular wheel by bolts and clamps.

AC-347 3½-Inch Guide Bands

Guide bands 3½ inches high are used in loose top soil conditions and for use on listed ridges. AC-407—Special guide band 4 inches high for listed rows, is also furnished and can be used alone or in connection with AC-347.

AC-180 Rear Wheel Scrapers

In soil that clings badly to wheels, filling up between the lugs and destroying traction, rear wheel scrapers are needed. Rear wheel scrapers can be used with spade lugs only.

AC-412 Extension Wheel Scrapers

Extension wheel scrapers—for use when 6½-inch extension rims are used. Attached with AC-180 described above.

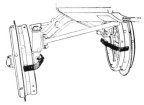

AC-247 Front Wheel Scrapers

To secure even depth in planting and cultivating, front wheels must be kept clean. In sticky soil, scrapers are therefore necessary. These scrapers are easily attached and are adjustable.

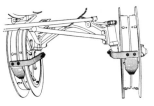

AC-590 Scraper for Double Front Wheel Guide Bands

Double guide bands on front wheels are found desirable when operating tractor on listed ridges. Scraper prevents guide bands from filling up in sticky soil, thereby maintaining their original effectiveness.

D-566 Canvas Engine Cover

Affords protection from the weather when tractor is left outside. Prevents theft of parts and tampering by unauthorized persons.

Used as shown on tractors No. 222802 and below. On later tractors it is necessary to remove auxiliary air cleaner and spark arrester.

The John Deere General Purpose TWO-CYLINDER Tractor

Model GP Special Equipment listing.

Special Equipment

AC-280 Citrous Grove Fenders

Attached over regular fenders and extends to hub of drive wheel to prevent damage to ends of vines and boughs through becoming entangled in spokes of wheel.

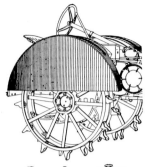

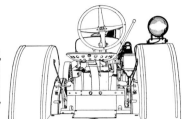

AC-425 Lighting Equipment

Lighting equipment can be furnished when it is desired to operate the tractor at night. The adjustable front light illuminates ahead of the tractor and the rear light illuminates the drawn machine. The current for lighting is supplied by a generator operated by a belt as shown in illustration above.

AD-677 Prest-O-Lite Lighting Equipment consists of a gas tank, head-lamp, rear lamp, brackets, tubing and attaching clips. This provides lighting equipment at low first cost. However, gas tanks must be refilled as the gas in the tank becomes exhausted.

AD-103 Exhaust Muffler

Used when horses or wagon loads of grain have to pass close to the tractor. Attached with clamp. Used on tractor No. 222802 and below. Muffler and spark arrester regular equipment on later tractors.

AD-241 Exhaust Elbow

Adjustable so that exhaust blast can be turned in any desired direction. Attached with clamp. Used on tractor No. 222802 and below. Muffler and spark arrester regular equipment on later tractors.

AC-435 Radiator Curtain

Adjustable to shut off any amount of air. Permits running the engine at best operating temperature in cold weather. Used on tractor No. 222802 and below. Regular equipment on later tractors.

AC-236 Radiator Guard

Substantially made in one piece. Will prevent cornstalks and brush from bending fins and will keep chaff and leaves from clogging air passages. Used on tractor No. 222802 and below. Regular equipment on later tractors.

AC-410 Muffler and Spark Arrester

This materially reduces exhaust sound of the engine and also prevents the escape of sparks, which is especially advantageous when tractor is operated in dry grain fields or around farm buildings. It attaches to the regular exhaust pipe. Used on tractor No. 222802 and below. Muffler and spark arrester regular equipment on later tractors.

AC-560 Air Cleaner with Vertical Auxiliary

For use on General Purpose Tractors prior to No. 212555. Used to provide oil filter cleaner with special vertical auxiliary cleaner.

AD-343 Auxiliary Air Cleaner

Auxiliary air cleaner for use in extremely dusty conditions. Removes 80 to 90 per cent of dust before air reaches regular oil filter cleaner. Used on tractor No. 222802 and below. Regular equipment on later tractors.

AC-580 Drawbar Shifter

Position of drawbar can be easily and quickly changed from the operator's seat without stopping tractor — of great advantage in sidehill plowing.

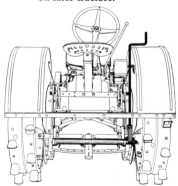

The Economical Tractor That Burns Low-Cost Fuel

Model GP Special Equipment listing.

The Farmall was heavier, longer, wider, and offered greater ground clearance than did the Standard GP. Its tricycle front end traveled between rows. Its rear wheels, set 74in apart, could straddle two rows. Its front-mounted cultivators worked either two or four rows at a time.

In conclusion, while the Standard Model GP was not a bad tractor, it was perhaps a better tractor in its other versions. Through the course of its production, modifications made the GP more competitive with the Farmall. Yet, in the end, GP sales remained meager in comparison.

Specifications: John Deere Standard Model GP

Horsepower	Suitable for two 14in plows or 22in thresher
Rating	10hp at drawbar, 20hp at belt
Speeds	Low, 2$\frac{1}{3}$mph; intermediate, 3$\frac{1}{8}$mph; high, 4$\frac{1}{3}$mph; reverse, 2mph
Engine	5$\frac{3}{4}$x6in bore and stroke, 950rpm, two-cylinder L-head type horizontal
Crankshaft	3in diameter, drop-forged, long bearings
Connecting rods	Drop-forged, two-bolt type
Lubrication	Force-feed, geared pump
Carburetor	Double-nozzle type with air choker
Air cleaner	Oil-filter type with auxiliary twister cleaners ahead
Ignition	High-tension magneto with enclosed impulse starter
Cooling	Tubular radiator, thermo-siphon
Air fan	Gear-driven, no belts
Governor	Enclosed, fly-ball type
Clutch	10in dry disks, locking in and out
Belt pulley	13in diameter, 6$\frac{1}{2}$in face, 950rpm
Belt speed	3,200fpm
Transmission	Spur gear, selective type, three speeds forward, one speed reverse
Gears	Forged-steel, cut, and heat-treated
Drive axle	2$\frac{1}{2}$in diameter, high-carbon steel
Drive wheels	42$\frac{3}{4}$x10in forged-steel rims
Front wheels	24x6in with dustproof bearings
Bearings	Main: 3$\frac{1}{4}$in long, removable, bronze-backed, Babbitt-lined
	Connecting rod: 2$\frac{3}{4}$in long, removable, bronze-backed, Babbitt-lined
	Front wheels and rear axles: Tapered roller (8) front axle, ball thrust (2)
	Transmission and belt pulley: Roller (1), ball (4), tapered roller (2)
	Fan and governor shaft: Ball (4), ball thrust (1)
Fuel tank capacity	Kerosene: 15 gallons
	Gasoline: 1$\frac{1}{2}$ gallons
Water capacity	9 gallons
Length with fenders and platform	112in
Width	59in
Height	56in at radiator cap
Turning radius	8ft
Drawbar height	Adjustable, vertical, 4$\frac{1}{2}$in; horizontal, 34$\frac{1}{2}$in
Drawbar clearance in high position	13in
Weight	3,600lb with 4in lugs, 2in guide bands, no fuel or water
Platform clearance	22in
Front axle clearance (center)	24in
Wheelbase	70$\frac{1}{2}$in
Rear wheel tread	49$\frac{1}{2}$in (center to center)
Power takeoff speed	For front or rear connections rotates clockwise, 520rpm; separate gear shift

Source: Deere Publication Series A144 of 1929.

Specifications: John Deere Standard Model GP

Horsepower	Suitable for two plows, 22in thresher, or 24in John Deere thresher
Speeds	Low, $2^{1}/_{4}$mph; intermediate, 3mph; high, 4mph; reverse, $1^{3}/_{4}$mph
Engine	6x6in bore and stroke, 950rpm, two-cylinder L-head type horizontal
Crankshaft	3in diameter, drop-forged, long bearings
Connecting rods	Drop-forged, two-bolt type
Lubrication	Force-feed, geared pump
Carburetor	Double-nozzle type with air choker
Air cleaner	Oil-filter type with vertical auxiliary cleaner
Ignition	High-tension magneto with enclosed impulse starter
Cooling	Tubular radiator, thermo-siphon
Air fan	Gear-driven, no belts
Governor	Enclosed, fly-ball type
Clutch	10in dry disks, locking in and out
Belt pulley	13in diameter, $6^{1}/_{2}$in face, 950rpm
Belt speed	3,200fpm
Transmission	Spur gear, selective type, three speeds forward, one speed reverse
Gears	Forged-steel, cut, heat-treated, and hardened
Drive axle	$2^{1}/_{2}$in diameter, high-carbon steel
Drive wheels	$42^{3}/_{4}$x10in forged-steel rims
Front wheels	24x6in with dustproof bearings
Bearings	Main: $3^{5}/_{8}$in long, removable, bronze-backed, Babbitt-lined
	Connecting rod: $2^{3}/_{4}$in long, removable, bronze-backed, Babbitt-lined
	Front wheels and rear axles: Tapered roller (8) front axle, ball thrust (2)
	Transmission and belt pulley: Roller (1), ball (4), tapered roller (2)
	Fan and governor shaft: Tapered roller (4), ball thrust (1)
Fuel tank capacity	Kerosene: 16 gallons
	Gasoline: 2 gallons
Water capacity	9 gallons
Length with fenders and platform	112in
Width	60in
Height	56in at radiator cap
Turning radius	8ft
Drawbar height	Adjustable, up and down, $4^{1}/_{2}$in; sideways, $34^{1}/_{2}$in.
Drawbar clearance in high position	13in
Weight	Approximately 3,750lb with 4in lugs, 2in guide bands, no fuel or water
Platform clearance	22in
Front axle clearance (center)	$22^{1}/_{2}$in
Wheelbase	$70^{1}/_{2}$in
Rear wheel tread	$49^{5}/_{8}$in (center to center)
Power takeoff speed	For front or rear connections rotates clockwise, 520rpm; separate gear shift

Source: Deere specification sheet of 1931.

Specifications: John Deere General Purpose Wide-Tread Model

Horsepower	Suitable for two 14in plows, 22in two- or four-row planter or cultivator in 36 or 38in rows, two-bottom lister or bedder.
Speeds	Low, $2^{1}/_{4}$mph; intermediate, 3mph; high, $4^{1}/_{8}$mph; reverse, $1^{3}/_{4}$mph
Engine	$5^{3}/_{4}$x6in bore and stroke, 950rpm, two-cylinder L-head type horizontal
Crankshaft	3in diameter, drop-forged, long bearings
Connecting rods	Drop-forged, two-bolt type
Lubrication	Force-feed, geared pump
Carburetor	Double-nozzle type with air choker
Air cleaner	Oil-filter type with vertical air stack
Ignition	High-tension magneto with enclosed impulse starter
Cooling	Tubular radiator, thermo-siphon
Air fan	Gear-driven, no belts
Governor	Enclosed, fly-ball type
Clutch	10in dry disks, locking in and out
Belt pulley	13in diameter, $6^{1}/_{2}$in face, 950rpm
Belt speed	3,200fpm
Transmission	Spur gear, selective type, three speeds forward, one speed reverse
Gears	Forged-steel, cut, and heat-treated
Final drive	Enclosed roller chains
Drive axle	$2^{1}/_{2}$in diameter, high-carbon steel
Drive wheels	$43^{1}/_{2}$in diameter
Front wheels	27x$4^{1}/_{2}$in concave face (reversible type)
Bearings	Main: $3^{1}/_{4}$in long, removable, bronze-backed, Babbitt-lined
	Connecting rod: $2^{3}/_{4}$in long, removable, bronze-backed, Babbitt-lined
	Front wheels and rear axles: Tapered roller (8), front bolster tapered roller (2)
	Transmission and belt pulley: Roller (1), ball (4), tapered roller (2)
	Fan and governor shaft: Tapered roller (4), ball thrust (1)
Fuel tank capacity	Kerosene: 16 gallons
	Gasoline: 2 gallons
Water capacity	9 gallons
Length	Overall, $117^{1}/_{2}$in
Width	$85^{1}/_{2}$in
Height	58in at radiator cap
Drawbar height	Adjustable, vertical, $5^{1}/_{2}$in; horizontal, 36in
Drawbar clearance in high position	12in
Wheelbase	$78^{5}/_{16}$in
Rear wheel tread	76in (center to center)
Power takeoff speed	For front or rear connections rotates clockwise, 520rpm; separate gear shift

Source: Deere specification sheet of 1930.

Specifications: John Deere General Purpose Wide-Tread Series P Model

Horsepower	Suitable for two 14in plows, or 22in thresher
Speeds	Low, 2$\frac{1}{4}$mph; intermediate, 3mph; high, 4$\frac{1}{8}$mph; reverse, 1$\frac{3}{4}$mph
Engine	5$\frac{3}{4}$x6in bore and stroke, 950rpm, two-cylinder L-head type horizontal
Crankshaft	3in diameter, drop-forged, long bearings
Connecting rods	Drop-forged, two-bolt type
Lubrication	Force-feed, geared pump
Carburetor	Double-nozzle type with air choker
Air cleaner	Oil-filter type with vertical air stack
Ignition	High-tension magneto with enclosed impulse starter
Cooling	Tubular radiator, thermo-siphon
Air fan	Gear-driven, no belts
Governor	Enclosed, fly-ball type
Clutch	10in dry disks, locking in and out
Belt pulley	13in diameter, 6$\frac{1}{2}$in face, 950rpm
Belt speed	3,200fpm
Transmission	Spur gear, selective type, three speeds forward, one speed reverse
Gears	Forged-steel, cut, and heat-treated
Final drive	Enclosed roller chains
Drive axle	2$\frac{1}{2}$in diameter, high-carbon steel
Drive wheels	44in diameter, 8in face
Front wheels	24x4in face
Bearings	Main: 3$\frac{1}{4}$in long, removable, bronze-backed, Babbitt-lined
	Connecting rod: 2$\frac{3}{4}$in long, removable, bronze-backed, Babbitt-lined
	Front wheels and rear axles: Tapered roller (8), front bolster tapered roller (2)
	Transmission and belt pulley: Roller (1), ball (4), tapered roller (2)
	Fan and governor shaft: Tapered roller (4), ball thrust (1)
Fuel tank capacity	Kerosene: 16 gallons
	Gasoline: 2 gallons
Water capacity	9 gallons
Length	Overall, 118$\frac{1}{2}$in
Width	76in
Height	57$\frac{1}{2}$in at radiator cap
Drawbar height	Adjustable, vertical, 5$\frac{1}{2}$in; horizontal, 36in
Drawbar clearance in high position	12$\frac{1}{2}$in
Wheelbase	78$\frac{1}{4}$in
Rear wheel tread	68in (center to center)
Power takeoff speed	For front or rear connections rotates clockwise, 520rpm; separate gear shift

Chapter 5

John Deere Model A

The Great Depression of the 1930s had a negative impact on agriculture, as it did on all sectors of the US economy. Between 1929 and 1932, total US cash farm income fell by nearly 60 percent. The drastic reduction in income left many farmers unable to cover their debt repayments. Consequently, between 1930 and 1934, 750,000 US farms changed ownership through foreclosure or bankruptcy sales.

Tractor Production and Sales 1924–1934

Year	Production	US sales	Export sales
1924	119,305	99,011	25,622
1925	167,553	121,998	45,924
1926	181,995	126,725	47,726
1927	200,504	160,637	42,132
1928	175,934	103,893	48,276
1929	228,976	160,0420	51,900
1930	202,458	132,749	44,185
1931	71,704	na	na
1932	20,000 (est.)	19,000 (est.)	na
1933	35,000 (est.)	na	na
1934	50,000 (est.)	na	na

Source: *Farm Implement News*, July 2, 1931, and other sources.

Percentage of Tractor Sales by Manufacturer (1935)

Manufacturer	Percentage of sales
International Harvester Co.	49.5%*
Deere and Co.	24.5*
Allis-Chalmers Manufacturing Co.	9.5
J. I. Case Co.	7.1
Oliver	3.6
Minneapolis-Moline	3.6
Massey-Harris Co.	0.7
Others	1.5

Source: Federal Trade Commission Report on the Agricultural Implement and Machinery Industry: Concentration and Competitive Methods.

The Depression also took its toll on the farm equipment industry. The manufactured value of implements and machinery plummeted from a record high of $512,936,000 in 1929, to $167,497,367 in 1931. By 1932, 92 percent of all farm equipment manufacturers reported a deficit, with aggregate industry losses of $50,000,000.

US tractor production had climbed steadily between 1922 and 1929. In 1929, industry production hit a high of 228,976 units. However, production slipped 12 percent in 1930 and plunged a further 65 percent in the following year.

As the chart shows, in 1932, US tractor production bottomed out at around 20,000 units, the lowest level since 1915.

Reportedly, 186 US companies manufactured farm tractors in 1921. By 1929, competition reduced the number of manufacturers to forty-seven. By 1933, fewer than twenty companies remained in the market, of which seven controlled 98.5 percent of wheel tractor production by 1935.

Deere and Company survived the Depression, but sales and profits collapsed. Although the company had manufactured tractors for little more than a decade, by the 1930s they accounted for 40 percent of Deere's profits.

As noted, hard times stifled tractor sales. Model D sales fell to 331 units in 1932 and Model GP sales, already below expectations, declined even further. Between 1929 and 1932, company

Deere and Co. Sales and Profits 1929–1933

Year	Sales	Profits/Losses*
1929	$76,000,000	$16,000,000
1930	63,000,000	7,600,000
1931	27,700,000	(1,000,000)
1932	8,700,000	(5,700,000)
1933	9,000,000	(4,300,000)

Source: *John Deere's Company: A History of Deere & Company and Its Times*, by Wayne G. Broehl, Jr., and other sources.

Note: Losses are shown in parentheses.

sales fell by 89 percent while profits declined by 135 percent.

Commitment to Product Development

Given the financial losses suffered by Deere, it was remarkable that the company proceeded to develop and introduce two new tractors, the Model A and Model B.

It was Charles Deere Wiman who compelled the board of directors to permit the continued cultivation of new products, despite "red ink," production scalebacks, and employee layoffs.

As Broehl wrote, "It is likely that the company would not have taken the steps to initiate these two new models ('A' and 'B') had it not been for Charles Wiman. . . . The expenditures made in that uneasy period were substantial. . . . It was a gamble by Wiman that was based upon faith and sound judgment. . . ."

Wiman took the helm as company president in October 1928, after William Butterworth left to become president of the United States Chamber of Commerce. Within a year, the stock market crashed and the world's economies were in a tailspin.

While Wiman curtailed some experimental programs, he did not cut back on tractor development. By 1931, Theo Brown's group was hard at work developing two new models.

Introduction of the Model A

First produced in 1933 as the Model AA, the tractor was field tested in Arizona's Salt River Valley, modified, and reintroduced a year later as the Model A. It went on to become the second most successful tractor in the history of Deere and Company. Full-scale production of the A Series began at the Waterloo tractor plant in April 1934 and ended in May 1953.

Available in a variety of configurations, the A Series' most innovative features included an adjustable rear axle (all versions except the AR, AO,

Styled version of the Model A; May 1938. Deere Archives

Pulley-side view of unstyled Model A. Deere and Co.

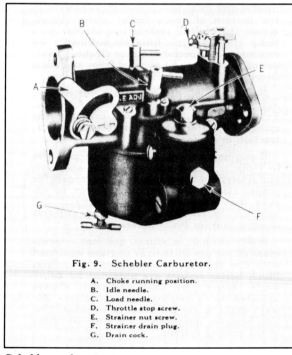

Fig. 9. Schebler Carburetor.

A. Choke running position.
B. Idle needle.
C. Load needle.
D. Throttle stop screw.
E. Strainer nut screw.
F. Strainer drain plug.
G. Drain cock.

Schebler carburetor.

and AO Streamlined); centerline hitch and PTO, and the first fully hydraulic power lift system.

The A Series styling was updated in the late 1930s; the difference is denoted by use of the characterizations "unstyled" and "styled." Another cosmetic make-over, carried out in 1949, affected a limited range of tractors that are referred to as "late styled" models. More than 327,000 units had been built by the end of the A Series' hugely successful nineteen-year production run.

Models FX and GX

The experimental Models FX and GX embodied many of the concepts that were incorporated into both the Model A and its smaller counterpart, the Model B.

The FX made its first appearance in the spring of 1932, and the GX followed in the fall of that same year. The FX bore a close resemblance to the GP Wide-Tread, with a similar cast-iron frame, radiator, and steering assembly. The FX was easily distinguished, however, by its adjustable rear axle and its overhead-valve engine.

The GX featured a different radiator and revamped steering assembly, as well as a fabricated iron frame. According to the Two-Cylinder, the GX was less complicated in design than the FX and more closely resembled the early Model A.

Models AA-1 and AA-3

The first production units were designated Models AA-1 and AA-3. The company authorized production and sale of ten tractors. However, only eight were built between April 8 and June 10, 1933: six units of the Model AA-1, which featured a four-speed transmission; and two of the Model AA-3, which was fitted with a three-speed transmission.

In July 1933, on the basis of field trials, it was decided that the Model AA-3 would be dropped. Production of the four-speed Model AA-1 was initiated in April 1934, at serial number 410,012.

Overview of the Model A

As mentioned, the Model A was produced in unstyled and styled versions, with four- and six-speed transmissions, and with distillate-burning ("all-fuel") and gasoline-burning engines.

Over the course of its production, nine distinct configurations were offered for agricultural applications:
• The two-wheel tricycle-front, itself referred to as the Model A
• The standard-front Model AR
• The wide-front Model AW
• The orchard version Model AO
• The one-wheel narrow-front Model AN
• The streamlined orchard version Model AOS
• The high-crop version of the Model AN, the Model ANH
• The high-crop version of the Model AW, the Model AWH
• The later high-crop version, Model AH.

A tenth configuration, the Model AI, was an industrial version. Its story is not part of this book, however.

The A Series Engine

Deere was firmly committed to its two-cylinder engine. Of the seven major manufacturers of general-purpose tractors, Deere alone employed a two-cylinder motor. Its simplicity, accessibility, greater economy, and longer life were qualities the company promoted for four decades.

The basic features of the A Series engine remained the same throughout its production run. Like the GP's engine, it was a horizontal design mounted crosswise on the frame, with its flywheel on the left-hand side of the tractor.

But unlike the GP's engine, whose flat-head, valve-in-block design was considered by some to have been outdated, the A Series engine featured the more popular valve-in-head design.

At introduction, the engine's bore and stroke measured 5½x6½in. Inlet and exhaust port diameters were 1⅞ and 1⅝in, respectively.

Lubrication was by gear-driven oil pump. The engine was cooled by a gear-driven fan that pulled air through a tubular radiator. No water pump was employed with its thermo-syphon system. Early models had an exposed shaft that drove the fan. Beginning with serial number 414,809, the shaft was enclosed.

Spark was generated by a Fairbanks-Morse Model DRV-2A magneto. The carburetor was a Schebler Model DLTX-8 double-nozzle type with air choke. The air intake was fitted to the left-hand side of the engine, with the exhaust stack on the right. Both stacks passed through the hood.

Vortex Air Cleaner

The early Model A was fitted with a vortex-type air cleaner, a filter-cleaner body assembly that incorporated a fine metal screen and an oil-filled, removable cup.

Air was drawn through the intake stack and entered the air cleaner body in the space between the cup of oil and the metal filter. Suction caused the air in the body to swirl and pick up oil from the cup. The mixture of oil and swirling air created a vortex, much like a whirlpool. The air and oil were pulled into the filter by the continued suction of the motor. The oil trapped dust and dirt particles, which could not pass through the mesh. The filtered, clean air was then sucked into the carburetor.

When the engine was shut off and the suction stopped, warm oil drained out of the filter and "thus [washed] any dirt down into the filter base."

The operators manual suggested that the cup be removed daily, at a minimum. The oil sediment or residue was scraped out of the cup, which was then cleaned with gasoline or distillate, refilled with oil, and replaced on the bottom of the cleaner assembly.

The vortex-type air cleaner was commonly used by engine manufacturers of the day.

Early A Series Engine Rating

The A Series engine was fitted with a variable-speed, centrifugal-type governor set to maintain engine speed at 975rpm under load.

In its Nebraska test of April 19–27, 1934 (Official Tractor Test No. 222), the engine generated 23.63hp at the belt pulley and 16.31hp at the drawbar, operating under rated load. Improved performance followed in 1941, when an engine with longer stroke was introduced.

A More Powerful Engine Is Produced

A new engine, with bore and stroke of 5½x6¾in, was tested at Nebraska in 1939 (Official

Tractor Test No. 335, November 13–16, 1939). It featured larger inlet and exhaust port diameters of 1⁵/₁₆ and 1⁴⁹/₆₄in, respectively.

Engine lubrication was by gear-driven oil pump, filtered through a partial-flow, replaceable, impregnated paper filter element positioned in the crankcase. The engine was cooled by the same thermo-syphon system employed on earlier models.

Spark was generated by a Wico magneto, Model C-1042. The carburetor was a Schebler Model DLTX-24, a "natural-draft" type with load and idle adjustment. The air intake and exhaust were fitted inline and through the hood, with the intake stack positioned closest to the operator.

In its official test, the Model A's larger engine generated 26.33hp at the belt and 20.12hp at the drawbar. These results reflected a horsepower increase of 23 percent at rated load.

Oil-Wash Air Cleaner

With the introduction of the larger engine, the vortex-type air cleaner used on the early Model A was replaced with a crimped-wire "oil-washed" United air cleaner.

With the oil-wash system, incoming air was drawn down the inlet stack and carried to an oil bath at the base of the reservoir. The oil and air were pulled up into a wire mesh filter element that surrounded the center inlet. Dirt- and dust-laden oil was trapped in the wire mesh filter element, as clean air was sucked into the carburetor.

A constant circulation of oil carried dirt to the base of the reservoir, where it settled. The operators manual recommended that the oil sediment cup be removed, cleaned, and rinsed in distillate or kerosene, and filled with new engine oil every ten hours, at a minimum.

Third Official Nebraska Test

Between October 27 and November 3, 1941, an official test of the Model AR was carried out at the University of Nebraska (Official Tractor Test No. 378). Although a six-speed transmission was introduced as standard equipment in 1941, the unit tested—serial number 584,043—was a four-speed version.

Fitted with a Marvel-Schebler Model DLTX-41 carburetor, the engine was basically the same as that of the tractor tested in November 1939. The

Unstyled Model A and Dain pickup baler; July 1936.
Deere Archives

report did indicate a change in oil filter element to a Purolator impregnated, replaceable paper full-flow filter with bypass. In this test, the AR's engine was rated at 26.30hp at the pulley and 20.25hp at the drawbar.

The Models A and AR were each tested once more at the Nebraska test facilities. Both units were fitted with the high-compression gasoline engine introduced by Deere in 1947, and matched with a six-speed transmission.

Deere's High-Compression Engine

Two significant factors influenced Deere and Company's decision to introduce a high-compression version of the two-cylinder engine. The first factor was the decrease in the cost of gasoline and the disappearance of low-grade distillates.

In 1937, the US farmer paid an average price of $0.11 per gallon for gasoline, whereas kerosene sold at $0.09 per gallon, and number two distillate cost as little as $0.06 per gallon. By the end of World War II, the petroleum industry had made significant advances in refining oil. Thus, the cost of producing gasoline fell more in line with that of kerosene.

As demand for distillate fuels declined, their prices increased and they no longer offered a significant price advantage. Eventually, low-grade distillates disappeared completely, which left kerosene as the primary alternative fuel source to gasoline.

The second factor that led to production of a more powerful two-cylinder was the demand for greater horsepower. As farmers brought more acreage into production, they sought larger tractors and implements. By the 1940s, when four-, six-, and eight-cylinder engines were commonplace (not to mention the magnificent twelve- and sixteen-cylinder engines of the previous decade), Deere's two-cylinder engine was an anomaly.

The demand for greater horsepower had escalated, and Deere's low-compression, distillate-burning, two-cylinder engine could not be coaxed to produce a significantly greater amount of power than it did in the version tested at Nebraska in November 1941. So rather than introduce a larger engine, Deere increased the existing motor's compression, which resulted in a more productive conversion of gasoline energy. The result was a greater output of horsepower.

The compression ratio in the new high-compression engine was raised from 4.45:1 for the all-fuel-burning engine, to 5.60:1 for the new gasoline engine. Compression pressure at cranking speed was raised from 75 to 110psi.

Two Final Tests at Nebraska

Between June 7 and 16, 1947, the Model A with high-compression gasoline engine and six-speed transmission was tested at Nebraska (Official Tractor Test No. 384). The engine was fitted with a Wico Model C-1042B centrifugal, variable-speed

Unstyled Model A with overhead steering and exposed steering pedestal, with drawn Model CC Van Brunt cultivator; July 1937. Deere Archives

magneto and Marvel-Schebler Model DLTX-71 carburetor. Test results indicated 33.53hp at the pulley and 26.28hp at the drawbar, an increase of better than 27 percent over the all-fuel engine.

The final test of the A Series was carried out on a Model AR, and was conducted between October 11 and 15, 1949 (Official Tractor Test No. 429). Fitted with electric start, twelve-volt Delco-Remy electrics, and Marvel-Schebler DLTX-71 carburetor, the engine generated 33.24hp at the pulley and 26.12hp at the drawbar. These results were virtually identical to those of the previous test.

It should be noted that, beginning with the Nebraska test of November 1941, Deere tractors were fitted with rubber tires in place of steel wheels.

Steering and Transmission

The A Series employed an automotive-type worm-gear steering system. With the unstyled models, as with the GP Wide-Tread, the steering shaft with worm passed over the hood to the worm-gear housing that was mounted on a pedestal in front of the radiator.

When the A Series was redesigned, the front pedestal was covered by sheet metal. On the styled

Styled Model A sheet metal, and grille-enclosed radiator and front pedestal. Deere Archives

series, a portion of the steering shaft passed through the hood. Its connection to the worm-gear housing was hidden beneath the hood.

The transmission originally fitted to the A Series featured four forward speeds and one reverse speed: first gear, 2$\frac{1}{3}$mph; second, 3$\frac{1}{3}$mph; third, 4$\frac{3}{4}$mph; fourth, 6$\frac{3}{4}$mph; and reverse, 3$\frac{1}{2}$mph.

Deere replaced the four-speed transmission with a six-speed unit at the same time it introduced the 5$\frac{1}{2}$x6$\frac{3}{4}$in engine. A dual-shift system, the new transmission employed two levers, one to select from three forward speeds and reverse, and a second to select from "Hi" and "Lo" ranges.

The new transmission offered speeds of 2$\frac{1}{2}$mph in first gear; 3$\frac{1}{4}$mph in second; 4$\frac{1}{4}$mph in third; 5$\frac{1}{2}$mph in fourth; 7$\frac{1}{3}$mph in fifth; and a "road gear" of 12$\frac{1}{2}$mph in sixth gear.

The advent of a road gear, a higher speed for the purpose of driving on roads, followed the introduction of low-pressure tractor tires.

Low-Pressure Pneumatic Tires: Rubber versus Steel

For a number of years prior to the successful introduction of low-pressure tractor tires, solid rubber tires had been mounted to tractors sold for certain industrial and orchard operations. In addition, low-pressure "balloon" tires were available for use in landscaping and lawn maintenance operations such as golf courses, cemeteries, and sod farms.

As early as 1926, Pennsylvania State University had tested a "rubber-tired" wheel, a pneumatic tire not unlike a truck tire developed "in an attempt to secure a wheel suitable for hauling as well as for general field work."

The tire proved ineffective in comparison to steel wheels. The field test report offered no conclusions or recommendations. However, it aptly depicted the dilemma: "a wheel that gives good traction (steel) is usually too rough riding to be used on the road and may be too wide for the cultivation of certain crops. A wheel that rides smoothly on the road (rubber tire) will often pack the ground excessively and is likely to fail to provide sufficient traction for heavy field work."

Throughout the middle to late 1920s, work on tractor tire development was carried out by B.F. Goodrich Company, Goodyear Tire and Rubber Company, and Firestone but with little improvement in tire performance.

It was 1932 before a general-purpose rubber tractor tire was introduced. As reported in the November 30, 1935, issue of *Business Week,* "Firestone . . . met the problem of traction by providing a tread of extra tough rubber, with deep grooves between cross-bars. Open grooves, from the sides of the tire beyond the center of the tread, [provided] a self-cleaning feature. A double layer of gum-dipped cords [locked] the tread and cord body, [and added] further strength."

Advantages of Rubber

Goodyear and Goodrich soon followed Firestone, producing tractor tires of their own. Word of the new tires spread across North America as professional journals, rural newspapers, and popular farm magazines wrote continually of the advantages of rubber over steel.

According to all reports, tires made operation in a higher gear possible because they reduced the tractor's rolling resistance; cut fuel consumption 25 to 35 percent; resulted in more power at the drawbar, through the existing transmission and final drive; accelerated work by as much as 25 percent; accomplished more work in less time; permitted more kinds of work to be done; did less damage to turf, soil, and young row crops; did not throw dirt over small crops nor raise dust clouds; permitted movement of farm machinery over highways; rode more easily, with less operator fatigue; and reduced repair bills and lengthened tractor life.

While some farmers resisted the change to rubber tires and continued use of steel wheels, the overwhelming majority welcomed the change. In a survey of farmers carried out by the ASAE (Amer-

Farm Implement News *cover: stranger things indeed have happened.*

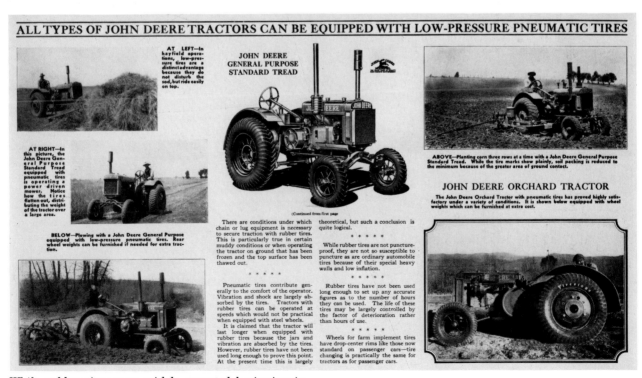

While rubber tires were widely accepted beginning in 1932, it was still necessary to promote their benefits. Deere Archives

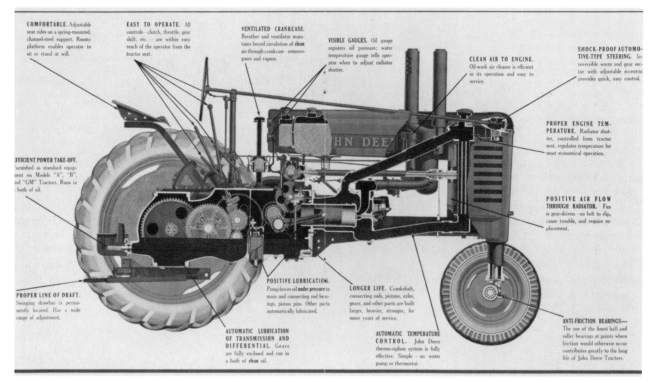

COMFORTABLE. Adjustable seat rides on a spring-mounted, channel-steel support. Roomy platform enables operator to sit or stand at will.

EASY TO OPERATE. All controls—clutch, throttle, gear shift, etc.— are within easy reach of the operator from the tractor seat.

VENTILATED CRANKCASE. Breather and ventilator maintains forced circulation of clean air through crankcase—removes gases and vapors.

VISIBLE GAUGES. Oil gauge registers oil pressure; water temperature gauge tells operator when to adjust radiator shutter.

CLEAN AIR TO ENGINE. Oil-wash air cleaner is efficient in its operation and easy to service.

SHOCK-PROOF AUTOMOTIVE-TYPE STEERING. Irreversible worm and gear sector with adjustable eccentric provides quick, easy control.

PROPER ENGINE TEMPERATURE. Radiator shutter, controlled from tractor seat, regulates temperature for most economical operation.

EFFICIENT POWER TAKE-OFF. Furnished as standard equipment on Models "A", "B", and "GM" Tractors. Runs in bath of oil.

POSITIVE AIR FLOW THROUGH RADIATOR. Fan is gear-driven—no belt to slip, cause trouble, and require replacement.

PROPER LINE OF DRAFT. Swinging drawbar is permanently located. Has a wide range of adjustment.

POSITIVE LUBRICATION. Pump forces oil under pressure to main and connecting rod bearings, piston pins. Other parts automatically lubricated.

LONGER LIFE. Crankshaft, connecting rods, pistons, axles, gears, and other parts are built larger, heavier, stronger, for more years of service.

ANTI-FRICTION BEARINGS— The use of the finest ball and roller bearings at points where friction would otherwise occur contributes greatly to the long life of John Deere Tractors.

AUTOMATIC LUBRICATION OF TRANSMISSION AND DIFFERENTIAL. Gears are fully enclosed and run in a bath of clean oil.

AUTOMATIC TEMPERATURE CONTROL. John Deere thermo-siphon system is fully effective. Simple — no water pump or thermostat.

Among other features, this cutaway shows the fully lubricated, all-gear final drive common to Model A and B tractors. Deere Archives

Rear view shows rear wheel tread set at narrowest position—56in. With inline PTO and hitch, this was the ideal width for plowing. Deere Archives

ican Society of Agricultural Engineers) in October 1934, more than 95 percent responded "yes" to the question, "If buying a new tractor, would you want it equipped with rubber tires?" It was an impressive response for a product that had been on the market for less than two years.

While only 5 percent of factory-delivered tractors were equipped with rubber tires in 1933, 45 percent were so equipped by 1935. In the same period, the market for farm tires grew from nothing to a $3.5 million yearly business. Within the next five years, 1.5 million tractors sported rubber as farmers retrofitted their existing tractors and tractor manufacturers universally adopted the rubber tire.

All-Gear Final Drive

Unlike the Model GP and Model D, for which power was transferred from the differential to the final drives via drive sprocket and roller chain, power for the A Series was transferred through forged-steel gearing. The exception was the A Series high-crop tractors, which used sprockets and double roller chain.

Adjustable Rear Wheel Tread

The A Series introduced the first adjustable rear wheel tread. While the rear tread width was fixed at 49½in on the Standard Model GP, and 76in

94

on the General Purpose Wide-Tread, the rear tread on the Model A was adjustable to any width between 56 and 84in.

When the rear wheels were placed on the axles with the hub bolts to the outside, the rear wheels were adjustable from 56 to 72in. When the wheels were reversed so that the hub bolts were on the inside, the rear wheels were adjustable from 68 to 84in.

Whether set at 56in for plowing, 68in for potato rows, 76in for cotton, or 80in for corn, the adjustable rear tread made the Model A adaptable to any type of work in rows spaced from 28 to 42in.

Improved Hitch and Power Shaft

The hitch on the Model A was located directly beneath the center of the axle housing. The drawbar was adjustable up, down, fore, aft, and sideways for convenience of attaching implements. With the rear tread set at 56in, the hitch on both

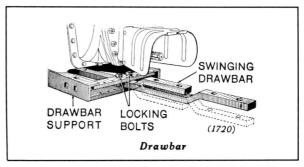

Drawbar hitch.

the tractor and drawn implement were centered, which largely overcame the problem of sidedraft.

The Model A was fitted with a power takeoff as standard equipment. Driven directly off the transmission, the shaft extended out of the center of the rear axle housing, which made it possible to attach

Rear wheel tread set at maximum of 88in. Deere Archives

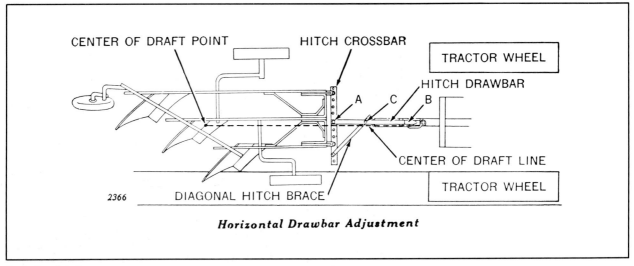

CENTER OF DRAFT POINT   HITCH CROSSBAR

TRACTOR WHEEL

HITCH DRAWBAR

A   C   B

CENTER OF DRAFT LINE

TRACTOR WHEEL

2366   DIAGONAL HITCH BRACE

Horizontal Drawbar Adjustment

Drawbar hitch.

PTO-driven implements in the center of the tractor.

The on-center hitch and PTO made drawn implements significantly easier to handle and greatly improved the performance of PTO-driven, drawn attachments.

Hydraulic Power Lift

The mechanical power lift of the General Purpose tractor was replaced with an optional hydraulic power lift on the A Series. It facilitated a quick, but cushioned drop of a mounted implement and could be operated while the tractor was either stationary or in motion.

Driven off the power takeoff shaft, it was necessary to engage the PTO before the lift was operated. Once engaged, all operations were controlled by either of two foot pedals.

Drawbar Performance

The Model A was a genuine two-plow tractor that complemented Deere's three-plow Model D. With its larger engine and greater horsepower rating, the Model A did not receive the same criticism as the Model GP.

Deere sales literature promoted the tractor as "designed to handle a six-horse load on drawbar jobs," and with its two- and four-row equipment "it put into the hands of one man the working capacity of three to six men using less modern equipment."

Its narrow, tapered hood permitted optimal forward view when cultivating. Its operator platform was sufficiently large and permitted the operator to stand for an even better view while running the machine (the Model A's hand-lever-engaged clutch and steering-column-mounted throttle lever permitted the operator to control the tractor from a standing position).

The Model A could easily handle two- and four-row operations. Its one-piece rear axle housing allowed for a high underaxle clearance. Its tricycle front and adjustable rear tread width made it an ideal row-crop unit.

In addition to a broad range of attachments that already existed, Deere complemented the A Series with several new implements. Among them were the GPA-102 Two-Row Integral Bedder, which could be converted into the GPA-103 Three-Row Integral Bedder for light work by adding a

On-center PTO and adjustable hitch were standard features of the Model A. Deere Archives

The PTO on the Model A powered the Model 6 combine; July 1937. Deere Archives

The Model A was rated as a two-plow tractor. Deere Archives

third beam; the Two-Row Planter Attachment for the GPA-102 and -103 bedders, which converted the bedder into a two-row planter or lister for cotton, corn, and other seeds; the GPA-140 Integral Two-

Row Middleburster and Lister; the Two-Row Planter Attachment for Middleburster; the GPA-402 Power-Lifted Four-Row Planter which permitted one operator to plant thirty-five to fifty

Hydraulic power lift facilitated operation of Dain push rake; July 1939. Deere Archives

Model A with integral disk plow; December 1939. Deere Archives

Model A and the Power-Trol hydraulically controlled land-leveler; June 1949. Deere Archives

Model A and Model 72 forage harvester; October 1950. Deere Archives

A styled Model A at work breaking soil. Deere Archives

Late Model A with Model 227 two-row corn picker. Deere Archives

acres a day in beds or in furrows; the GPA-477 Power-Lifted Four-Row Planter especially adapted for planting on loose or sandy beds, and on flat land; the GPA-260 Two-Row Cultivator (northern); the GPA-460 Four-Row Cultivator (northern); the

Studio photo of Model 15 mounted cotton harvester and late Model A; April 1952. Note starter, electric lights, and cushioned seat. Deere Archives

Wheel choices for the Model A included standard-lug steel wheel rears and steel-spoke front wheels. Deere Archives

GPA-270 Two-Row Cultivator (southern); and the GPA-470 Four-Row Cultivator (southern).

Throughout the life of the Model A, Deere continued to develop and redesign implements well suited to the tractor. An abbreviated list of model designations and descriptions follows.

Other types of equipment suited to the Model A included a sweep rake, beet harvester, fertilizer attachment, multi-row cotton and vegetable duster, power mower, one- and two-row corn picker, two-row cotton harvester, push-type manure loader, and stalk cutter.

A Series Special Equipment

At introduction, the Model A was available with either steel wheels or rubber tires. The standard steel drive wheels were 6x50in forged steel with twenty-four 4½in spade lugs. Either a spoked wheel or self-cleaning disk-type front wheel was available. The standard tires were 9x38in for the rear, and 6x16in for the front.

Optional wheel equipment included skeleton rear wheels; 4in and 6in extension rims suited to

Skeleton steel rear wheels were also available for the Model A, as were self-cleaning front wheels. Deere Archives

Steel-spoke wheels were optional on the Model A; May 1938. Deere Archives

Pressed-steel wheels, front and rear. Deere Archives

the steel drive wheels; front wheel extension rims; 5in spade lugs; 2½in front wheel guide bands; rear road band assembly, which bolted to the steel wheel and encompassed the wheel and lug for use when the tractor was driven on surfaced roads; and rear wheel button lugs and cast cone lugs.

Later wheel and tire options included a single steel front wheel, single front wheel with pneumatic tire (effectively the Model N); 5½x16in six-ply front tires mounted on cast- or pressed-steel wheels; 9x38in four- and six-ply rears mounted on steel-disk type or heavy-cast wheels; 10x38in four- and six-ply rears mounted on steel-disk or heavy-cast wheels; and 11x38in six-ply rears mounted on

Artwork shows the styled versions of the Models A and B—the work of Henry Dreyfuss. Deere Archives

heavy-cast wheels. A variety of wheel weights were also available.

Other options included adjustable rear fenders, lighting equipment, and in 1938, electric starting.

Styled Tractors and Other Modifications

During the 1930s, product design emerged as a critical concern to American manufacturers. Prior to this decade, the functional aspect of a product was foremost. If a device worked, about what should the manufacturer be concerned?

Style, perhaps?

By the mid-1930s, the US economy had strengthened and many companies turned their attention toward the issue of style.

To most of the population, the farm tractor was a functional tool that had merely replaced the horse as a source of power—a frame that supported a motor, drive gear, and two sets of wheels.

Oil pressure and water temperature gauges on styled tractors were simple and easily visible. Deere Archives

Nonetheless, a group of engineers at Deere and Company were determined to make the tractor more appealing to the eye.

Henry Dreyfuss was an internationally renowned leader in the flourishing field of industrial design. In 1937, Deere engineers turned to Dreyfuss to improve the styling of their tractors.

Dreyfuss redesigned Deere's tractors with two goals in mind: first, to improve their aesthetics; and second, to make them easier and less expensive to manufacture.

The Dreyfuss redesign took a little more than one year to execute. By the 1938 model year, styled versions of the Model A and B were ready for introduction.

The principal changes in the Model A included a metal cowling that covered the front steering pedestal and wrapped around the side and top of the radiator; a louvered radiator grille; a higher profile hood that enshrouded a good portion of the steering shaft; a new dash area; and repositioned intake and exhaust stacks, placed inline for a more streamlined look.

The styled version of the Model A had a much sleeker, more forceful appearance. The company promoted their newly restyled line as "tomorrow's tractors today."

Over the course of nearly two decades, a number of modifications and updates were made to the A Series tractors. Some of the more significant alterations included a change in 1934 from a triangular-shaped, straight frame brace beneath the engine to a dished brace that improved clearance for the integral cultivator. In 1935, the fuel spout was relocated from the center of the tank to left-of-center, which eliminated interference from the steering column. In 1937, a heavier clutch was installed along with a larger, twelve-spline axle.

In 1947 several changes occurred, including a pressed-steel frame; the Roll-O-Matic front end whose knee-action acted like an independent suspension system that transferred up-and-down movement equally between the two front wheels; electric starting and lights as standard equipment; Powr-Trol, a remote hydraulic system for drawn implements, was introduced; the battery was moved from beneath the hood to underneath the seat support; a cushioned operator seat with backrest was offered; and an optional split- or two-piece front pedestal was introduced which permitted interchangeable front ends—dual front, dual front with Roll-O-Matic, adjustable front (56 to 80in), and single front wheel for narrow-space rows such as vegetables.

Model AR: A Two-Plow Standard Tractor

The Model D was a popular tractor that, by 1935, had been in production for twelve years. A three-plow tractor with standard tread, it ably

Unstyled Model AR. Deere and Co.

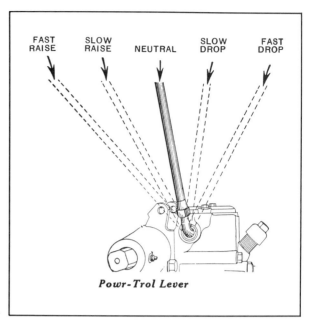

Powr-Trol remote hydraulic controls. Deere and Co.

handled applications that did not require a row-crop tractor.

With the introduction of the Model AR in 1935, Deere offered small-grain farmers a two-plow standard tractor with the versatility of the Model A. Promoted for its ability to do the work of a six-horse team, the Model AR's four-speed transmission offered 2mph and 3mph speeds for heavy drawbar work, as well as a road gear speed of 5⅓mph for transport work.

The Model AR was easily distinguished from the Model A by its fixed rear axle and its lack of overhead steering mechanism.

Model AR Modifications

The Model AR and its orchard companion the AO were the last A Series tractors removed from production. While production of the Models A, AN, and AW ceased by May 1952, the AR and AO were built for another year.

In 1949, Deere introduced the high-compression gasoline engine to the AR model. Subse-

This ad for standard tread tractors featured the Model AR. Deere Archives

Styled AW awaits restoration by the Keller family.

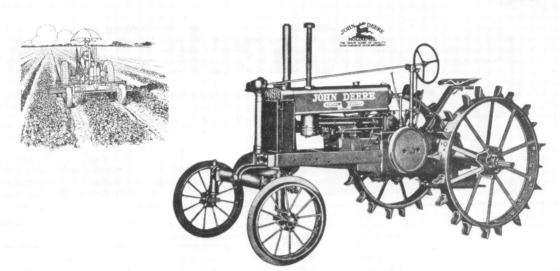

John Deere Models AW and BW Tractors

with Adjustable Tread in Front as Well as Rear

IN PLANTING and cultivating widely variable row crops, in bedded crops where it is desired to straddle the beds in planting and cultivating without splitting the center, in extremely soft and friable soils, you'll find no tractors better suited to your needs than the John Deere AW and BW Tractors with adjustable front tread.

Wide Distribution of Weight

The wide distribution of weight over four points of ground contact makes for more successful operation in the lighter soils—for safer handling across water furrows and dykes—for easier steering where the wheels can't ordinarily get a purchase.

Handle Variety of Row Crops

Practically all row crops can be handled with the adjustable front axle which can be pulled in to 56 inches or extended out to 80 inches in four-inch steps.

By moving out only one side at a time, two-inch increases in tread can also be secured.

The rear tread is also adjustable from 56 to 84 inches as on the standard Models A and B Tractors. This makes it possible for the front and rear wheels to track alike—an important point for a cultivating tractor in getting over soft muck lands and in straddling bedded crops without splitting the center of the bed.

See these new tractors. In speed, economy, capacity, effortless vision, centered hitch in plowing, these tractors are the same Models A and B which have been making such a phenominal performance record these past few years. The only change is that the front wheels are adjustable, the same as the rear.

Planting and Cultivating Equipment Available

The same planting and cultivating equipment—the AB Series—which fits the regular Models A and B will also fit these AW and BW Tractors.

In soil so friable that it is impossible to hold a furrow wall, the Model AW and BW Tractors operate successfully. There is wide distribution of weight.

Near Phoenix, Arizona. A Model BW, working in a field of cantaloupes. Fertilizer, previously applied, is being turned under and furrows prepared for irrigation.

Where conditions are particularly difficult, wheels can be equipped with extension rims. The tractor stays on top of soil as soft as that shown here.

The Model AW featured both adjustable front and rear axles. Deere and Co.

quently, the company had offered both the new engine and the all-fuel version.

The AR with the gasoline unit was rated as a standard three-plow tractor, while the all-fuel version was rated as a two-plow tractor. At nearly 35 drawbar hp, the gasoline unit easily rivaled the Model D in drawbar performance. Fewer than 600 units of the all-fuel AR were built. Consequently, they are highly valued among collectors.

While modifications to the AR's transmission and engine parallel those made to the Model A, its restyling was not carried out until 1949. When the Model AR was finally restyled it was done in the fashion of the Model R, Deere's first diesel-powered standard tractor, which was introduced that same year.

The restyled AR was never referred to as styled. Rather, it was marketed as the "New Improved 'AR' Tractor." Among collectors, it is referred to as late-styled.

According to an article in *Two-Cylinder*, modifications made to the late-styled AR included a perforated metal grille; tapered hood and fuel tank; crankcase ventilation, which replaced the old-style breather; twelve-volt starter and lighting; a six-speed transmission operated by a single lever; improved Powr-Trol remote hydraulics with increased lift capacity; optional heavy-duty drawbar; fully adjustable cushioned seat; re-grouped instruments and controls; and the option of a magneto in place of the standard distributor.

When production ended in May 1953, the Model AR was replaced by the Model 60 Standard.

Model AW Wide-Front

Introduced in 1935, the Model AW, which stood for wide-front, offered an adjustable front tread as well as an adjustable rear tread. It was designed for use in farming operations that produced widely varied row-crops; for bedded crops such as cantaloupe and other melons, where straddling the beds was preferred for planting and cultivating; and in extremely friable soils—soils that crumbled readily.

The weight of the AW was widely distributed over four points which, according to promotional literature, "[made] for more successful operation in the lighter soils—for safer handling across water furrows and dikes—for easier steering where wheels [couldn't] ordinarily get a purchase."

Production of the Model AW began in May 1935. The tractor was restyled at the same time as the Model A. Production of the AW was suspended in May 1952.

The Model AO was available on either steel wheels or rubber tires. Deere and Co.

AOS sheet metal protected the radiator, motor, and operator from branches.

Low-profile Model AOS operator platform. Deere and Co.

Models AO and AO Streamlined

The Model AO, a tractor for grove, orchard, and vineyard operations, was introduced in 1935. It shared many features with the Model AR, including its common steering mechanism. In 1936, the AO was offered with a streamlined front grille, hood, and full-skirted rear fenders. Redesignated the Model AO Streamlined, it remained in production through 1940.

The streamlined Model AOS was built from November 1936 to October 1940. Deere and Co.

The AO and AO Streamlined were low-profile tractors with exhaust that swept down below the hood line. Its lowered air intake, steering, and controls were designed not to catch on branches. Guards protected the gas and distillate tank caps. The lowered operator seat and platform were positioned so that the operator's head rose only slightly above the steering wheel.

The AO and AO Streamlined models were available with either steel drive wheels as standard equipment, or optional rubber tires. Rubber-tired models were fitted with solid cast-iron rear wheels, which eliminated spokes that could catch and damage branches and, in most cases, made wheel weights unnecessary.

Their low, compact design enabled the AO and AO Streamlined to get closer to trees, even when branches were trimmed low. Their independent brakes (common to all the A Series tractors) made short turns around trees possible.

The AO Streamlined was dropped in 1940, when the AO and AR were fitted with the $5\frac{1}{2}$x$6\frac{3}{4}$in engine. As stated, the AO and AR were not restyled until 1949, when they were restyled in the fashion of the Model R. Models AO and AR were built until May 1953. The AO was succeeded by the Model 60-O.

Model AN Narrow-Front

The Model AN, which stood for narrow-front, was introduced in 1935 and featured a single front wheel. It was the complement to the Model AW. In fact, the AW's adjustable front end could be interchanged with that of the AN, in a later version of the Model A that featured the two-piece front pedestal.

In narrow-row applications, such as commercial flower and vegetable farms, crops were grown in 12 to 16in spacings. The single front wheel of the Model AN could easily pass between rows, while its rear tread could be adjusted to suit a variety of row spacings.

The AN was available with either steel wheels or rubber tires. The drive wheel size was the same as that fitted to the Model A, while the single front wheel measured 24x8in.

Deere offered a variety of implements designed expressly for vegetable gardening, including planters and cultivators.

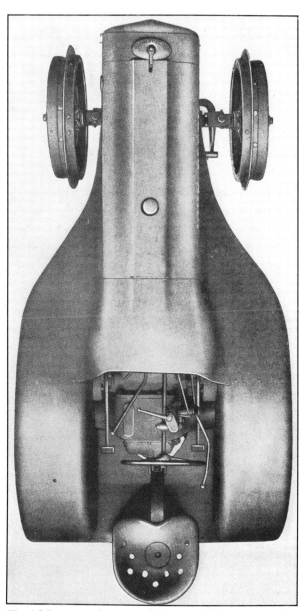

The AOS radiator was protected by its streamlined grille. Deere and Co.

The AOS tractor sheet metal protected driver and wheels from low-hanging branches. Deere and Co.

John Deere Models AN and BN Tractors
The Answer to the Narrow-Row Problem

THE John Deere Models AN and BN Tractors are identical to the Models A and B, previously described, except that they are equipped with a single front wheel (either steel or rubber tire).

The single front wheel runs between narrow rows, even where the distance between the rows is as narrow as 12 to 16 inches. This feature, together with the adjustable spacing of the rear wheels, narrow, compact design, light weight, and easy handling, makes these tractors the ideal power units for the commercial grower of vegetables or flowers.

Solves Horse Problem

All of the integral working equipment for the regular Models A and B can be used with these Models AN and BN tractors and, in addition, a complete line of special garden planters and cultivators is available. Thus, the owner of an AN or BN tractor can do away completely with the expense and inconvenience of horses. He is equipped to do the best possible job of plowing, preparing his seed bed, planting and cultivating. With four forward speeds, he can adapt the speed to the job, getting over the ground rapidly, taking advantage of the breaks in the weather, *doing each job at the time it should be done.*

If you have narrow rows to cultivate, investigate these tractors. Both tractors and equipment have undergone exhaustive field tests in a big variety of narrow and wide-row crops.

These special tractors can be equipped, as shown, with special rear wheels, low-pressure rubber tires, and special single front wheels with low-pressure tires or double low-pressure tires in front.

Good seed beds are easier to make with a BN tractor. Above view shows a Model BN plowing with a John Deere No. 51 Plow.

Planting six rows of vegetables with John Deere B-636 Garden Planter.

Cultivating young lettuce with John Deere B-514 Six-Row Power-Lift Cultivator. Taken near Phoenix, Arizona.

Single front wheel on Model AN easily ran between narrow-row vegetable crops. Deere and Co.

Production of the Model AN was suspended in May 1952.

Models ANH and AWH

The Models ANH and AWH were high-crop versions of the AN and AH models, respectively, and were used primarily in tall vegetable crops.

Built between 1937 and 1946, the tractors received the same restyling, larger engine, and six-speed transmission as were fitted to the Models A, AN, and AW.

Model AH

Introduced in 1950, the Model AH was a latecomer to the A Series. It was intended for use in crops such as sugar cane and pineapples, and was also sold for use in nursery operations.

Promoted as the "Famous Model 'A' on Stilts," it featured 32in ground clearance at the axles. At 97½in overall height, 152½in overall length, and weighing 6,400lb, the AH stood 16⅜in taller, stretched 18½in longer, and weighed 1,400lb more than the Model A.

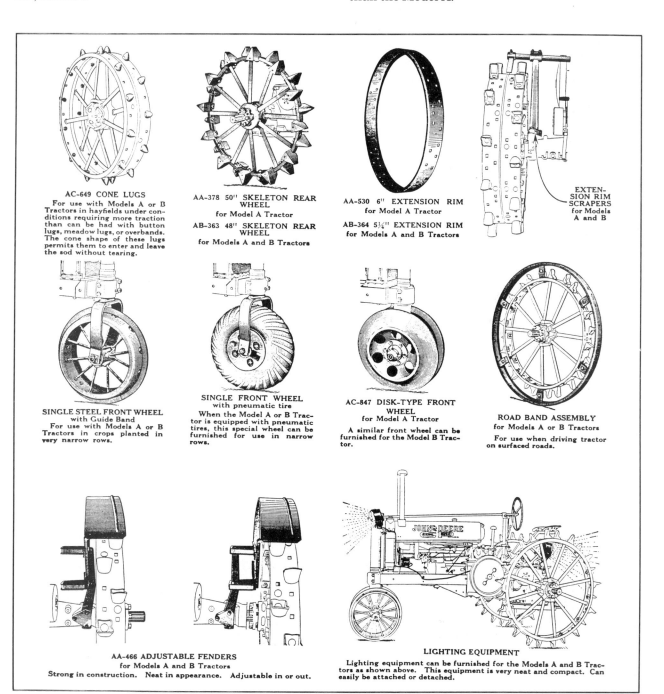

Model A Special Equipment listing.

The AH featured a choice of either the high-compression gas or all-fuel $5\frac{1}{2}$x$6\frac{3}{4}$in engines. It also featured overhead steering and was fitted with the six-speed, single-lever transmission.

The AH was built in limited numbers between July 1950 and April 1952.

Farewell to the Model A

Since the end of World War II, Deere had been under pressure to improve many aspects of their tractors.

Advancements had been made in tractor design that included independent power takeoff; improved hydraulics and hitches; duplex carburetion; and of course, more powerful four-cylinder gas motors and diesel engines.

To a large degree, Deere had responded to these demands through the introduction of the diesel-powered Model R, and the upright two-cylinder engine of the Model M. By the 1950s, however, the Models A and B were outdated tractors whose days were numbered. They could no longer be updated efficiently or effectively.

On May 6, 1953, production of the A Series was terminated, when the last units of Models AO and AR were built. Production of the Model A (the original tricycle-front configuration) had been terminated on May 12, 1952, two months after manufacture of the 60 Series had begun.

IHC versus Deere: Shares of Market 1921–1935

Product line	Market share		
	1921	**1929**	**1935**
Grain and rice binders			
IHC	73.2%	67.9%	67.2%
Deere	13.5	25.9	24.7
Combines, all widths			
IHC	85.1	31.8	32.4
Deere	na	6.8	15.6
Grain threshers			
IHC	4.6	26.7	15.8
Deere	na	na	4.8
Mowers, horse or tractor			
IHC	62.4	64.6	59.6
Deere	14.3	20.7	20.9
Rakes, sulky, dump			
IHC	51.2	56.2	52.4
Deere	14.7	20.8	20.8
Rakes, side delivery, combine rakes, and tedders			
IHC	53.3	62.9	40.8
Deere	25.7	22.8	26.2
Hay loaders, all types			
IHC	43.9	53.1	54.3
Deere	26.3	22.7	28.4
Corn binders			
IHC	70.1	68.8	54.3
Deere	17.3	22.2	29.7
Corn pickers, field, horse or tractor			
IHC	97.5	48.5	29.7
Deere	na	29.4	12.5
Walking plows, moldboard, one-horse			
IHC	2.9	11.0	7.9
Deere	na	na	na
Walking plows, moldboard, two-horse and larger			
IHC	8.4	14.5	20.7
Deere	10.4	12.6	13.0
Sulky plows, moldboard, horse-drawn, one-bottom and larger			
IHC	13.0	19.7	18.9
Deere	12.2	25.2	14.4
Tractor plows, moldboard, one-bottom and larger			
IHC	15.8	49.1	48.8
Deere	5.3	26.5	18.4
Disk harrows, horse and tractor			
IHC	32.2	41.8	35.9
Deere	17.9	22.4	22.4
Spike-tooth harrows, sections, steel and wood			
IHC	31.5	28.4	28.0
Deere	21.6	19.1	19.7
Spring-tooth harrows, sections			
IHC	27.1	34.6	29.0
Deere	19.4	24.5	18.4
Corn planters, two-row, horse or tractor			
IHC	32.3	32.0	34.9
Deere	25.0	41.2	37.3
Cultivators, walking, one-row, two-horse			
IHC	7.4	na	17.6
Deere	14.6	18.5	22.8
Cultivators, riding, one-row, two-horse			
IHC	34.8	44.8	40.1
Deere	18.7	20.1	21.5
Cultivators, riding, two-row, horse-drawn			
IHC	23.1	27.7	16.6
Deere	27.1	29.9	18.1
Cultivator, tractor-drawn or mounted			
IHC	—	83.8	56.1
Deere	—	10.3	21.1

Tractors, all-purpose, wheel type, all sizes

IHC	—	59.9	49.5
Deere	—	21.1	24.5

Engines, internal combustion, under 5hp, except marine

IHC	—	15.3	6.9
Deere	—	12.7	2.3

Source: Federal Trade Commission Report on the Agricultural Implement and Machinery Industry: Concentration and Competitive Methods.
Notes: Walking and riding cultivators were combined in IHC's report for 1929; total is reflected under riding cultivators. Also, dashes represent data not available.

Specifications: John Deere Model A General Purpose Tractor with Adjustable Tread

Horsepower	Two 14in plows, 22in thresher or 24in John Deere thresher, two- and four-row planter, or two- or four-row cultivator
Speeds	First, 2¹/₃mph; second, 3¹/₃mph; third, 4³/₄mph; fourth, 6³/₄mph; reverse, 3¹/₂mph
Engine	5¹/₂x6¹/₂in bore and stroke
Crankshaft	Main bearings 2³/₄x3¹/₄in; connecting rod bearings 3x2³/₈in
Carburetor	Double-nozzle type with air choker
Air cleaner	Oil-wash type with vertical air stack
Cooling	Tubular radiator, thermo-syphon
Air fan	Gear driven, no belts; 1903rpm, diameter 16¹/₂in
Governor	Enclosed fly-ball type
Clutch	10in dry disks, locking in and out
Belt pulley	13in diameter, 7¹/₂in face, 975rpm
Belt speed	3,270fpm
Transmission	Spur gear, selective type, four speeds forward, one speed reverse
Gears	Forged-steel, cut, and heat-treated
Final drive	Forged-steel, cut, and heat-treated
Drive axle	2⁷/₈in diameter
Bearings	Main: 2³/₄x3¹/₄in, bronze-backed, Babbitt-lined
	Connecting rod: 3x2³/₈in, diecast
	Camshaft, two taper roller
	Governor shaft, two ball
	Fan shaft, two ball
	Belt pulley, one bronze, one roller
	Front wheels and rear axle: Four taper roller
	Vertical steering spindle: Radax ball bearing at bottom, plain bearing at top
Transmission	a. Differential, two taper roller
	b. Spline shaft, two ball bearing
	c. Reverse shaft, none
Fuel tank capacity	Fuel: 14 gallons; Gasoline: 1 gallon
Water capacity	9¹/₂ gallons
Length	Overall, 124in
Width	86in
Height	60in at radiator cap
Turning radius	8ft
Drawbar height	Vertical adjustment 8 to 15in; horizontal 26¹/₂in
Wheelbase	87in
Rear wheel tread	56 to 80in
Weight	3,525lb
Power takeoff speed	536rpm

Source: Deere Publication Series A173 of 1933.

Specifications: John Deere Model A General Purpose Tractor with Adjustable Tread

Horsepower	Two 16in plow bottoms or a two-bottom bedder under normal conditions, and three 14in plow bottoms or a four-bottom bedder under favorable conditions
Speeds	First, 2¹/₂mph; second, 3¹/₄mph; third, 4¹/₄mph; fourth, 5¹/₂mph; fifth, 7¹/₃mph; sixth, 12²/₃mph; reverse, 4mph

Specifications: John Deere Model A General Purpose Tractor with Adjustable Tread

Belt pulley 12^3/$_4$in diameter; 7^3/$_8$in face, 975rpm, one roller and one bronze bearing

Belt speed 3,270fpm

Engine Two cylinders, cast-in-block, valves-in-head
Speed: 975rpm
Bore and stroke: 5^1/$_2$x6 ^{3}/$_4$in
Crankshaft: Special-quality steel, drop-forged, 3in crank pins
Main bearings: Two bronze-backed, Babbitt-lined, removable, 2^3/$_4$in diameter,
    3^1/$_4$in length
Connecting rods: Special-quality steel, drop forged; Babbitt bearings,
    centrifugally spun in rod,
3in diameter, 2^3/$_8$in width; bronze bushing for piston pin
Governor: John Deere design, enclosed fly-ball with one ball thrust and two self-
    adjusting ball bearings
Carburetor: Natural-draft type with load and idle adjustment
Ignition: High-tension magneto with enclosed automatic impulse starter
Air cleaner: Oil-wash type
Lubrication: Full force-feed pressure system with oil filter
Cooling: Thermo-siphon with gear- and shaft-driven fan (no belts or water
    pump)

Fuel tank capacity Fuel: 15 gallons
Gasoline: 1 gallon

Water capacity 9^1/$_4$ gallons

Clutch Two 10in dry disks, locking in and out

Transmission Selective type, spur gears, forged, cut, and heat-treated; four speeds forward,
    one speed reverse; shafts operating on two roller, four tapered, six ball
    bearings

Rear axles 2^3/$_4$in diameter; mounted on four tapered roller bearings

Rear wheels Tire sizes/wheel equipment:
9-38 four-ply pressed-steel
9-38 six-ply pressed-steel or cast
10-38 four-ply pressed-steel or cast
10-38* six-ply pressed-steel or cast
11-38 four-ply pressed-steel or cast
11-38 six-ply pressed-steel or cast
12-38 six-ply pressed-steel or cast
*Mounted on cast wheels; recommended for average field conditions.
Note: Cast wheels were approximately 265lb heavier than steel wheels. Steel-
    spoke wheels with lugs were available as special equipment. Diameter 50in,
    face 6in (furnished with four speeds only).

Front wheels 5.50x16in four-ply rubber tires; mounted on four tapered roller bearings; steel-
    spoke wheels with guide bands available as special equipment; 24in diameter,
    4in face

Rear wheel tread 56 to 84in

Wheelbase 90in

Turning radius 8ft, 7^1/$_2$in

Drawbar adjustment Vertical adjustment: 9^3/$_8$ to 18^1/$_8$in
Horizontal adjustment: 26^1/$_2$in
Lengthwise adjustment: 10^1/$_2$in

Power takeoff speed 546rpm

Dimensions Overall width: 83in
Overall length: 133^1/$_8$in
Overall height: 79^1/$_2$in
Height to radiator cap: 63^3/$_8$in

Shipping weight 4,351lb

Note: Dimensions and weight are based on 10-38 six-ply tires mounted on cast wheels.
Source: Deere Publication Series A456 of 1941.

Specifications: John Deere Model A General Purpose Tractor with Adjustable Tread

Horsepower
All-fuel economy engine: Maximum 26.83hp on the drawbar and 30.98 on the belt

Increased-compression gasoline engine: Maximum 35.30hp on the drawbar and 39.45 on the belt

Speeds
First, 2½mph; second, 3¼mph; third, 4¼mph; fourth, 5½mph; fifth, 7⅓mph; sixth, 12⅔mph; reverse, 4mph

Belt pulley
Regular equipment, 12¾in diameter; 7⅜in face, 975rpm

Belt speed
3,270fpm

Power takeoff speed
Conforms to ASAE power takeoff standards

Engine
Two cylinders, cast-in-block, valves-in-head

Speed: 975rpm

Bore and stroke: 5½x6¾in

Main bearings: Two steel-backed, Babbitt-lined, removable, 2¾in diameter, 3¼in length

Connecting rod bearings: Babbitt, centrifugally spun in rod, 3in diameter, 2⅜in width

Governor: John Deere design, enclosed fly-ball with one ball thrust and two self-adjusting ball bearings

Carburetor: Natural-draft type with load and idle adjustment

Ignition: High-tension magneto with enclosed automatic impulse starter

Air cleaner: Oil-wash type

Lubrication: Full force-feed pressure system with oil filter

Cooling: Thermo-siphon with gear- and shaft-driven fan (no belts or water pump)

Starting and lighting
Regular equipment; twelve-volt system with voltage regulator; two front lights and one rear light

Fuel tank capacity
All-fuel engine: 14 gallons, plus 1 gallon gasoline

Gasoline engine: 14 gallons

Water capacity
8¾ gallons

Clutch
Two 10in dry disks, locking in and out

Rear axles
2¾in diameter; mounted on four tapered roller bearings

Rear tires and wheels
11-38 six-ply, on cast or pressed-steel wheels

Front tires and wheels
5.50x16in four-ply; disk wheels reversible

Rear wheel tread
56 to 88in

Wheelbase
90in

Turning radius
8ft, 7½in

Drawbar adjustments
Conform to ASAE standards for drawbar hitch locations

Dimensions
Overall width: 87in

Overall length: 133⅛in

Overall height: 80in

Height to radiator cap: 64½in

Shipping weight
4,909lb with power lift and cast rear wheels

Source: Deere Publication Series A56 of 1947.

Specifications: John Deere Model AR Tractor

Horsepower
Drawbar load of six-horse team

Speeds
First, 2mph; second, 3mph; third, 4mph; fourth, 6¼mph; reverse, 3mph

Belt pulley
12¾in diameter; 7¼in face, 975rpm

Belt speed
3,270fpm

Engine
Two cylinders, cast-in-block, valves-in-head

Speed: 975rpm

Bore and stroke: 5½x6½in

Governor: Enclosed fly-ball type

Carburetor: Natural-draft type with load and idle adjustment

Ignition: High-tension magneto with enclosed automatic impulse starter

Specifications: John Deere Model AR Tractor

	Air cleaner: Oil-wash type with vertical air stack
	Lubrication: Full force-feed pressure system with oil filter
	Cooling: Thermo-siphon with gear- and shaft-driven fan (no belts or water pump)
Fuel tank capacity	Fuel: 16 gallons
	Gasoline: 1 gallon
Water capacity	8 gallons
Clutch	Two 10in dry disks, locking in and out
Transmission	Selective spur gear
Rear wheel size	42³⁄₄in diameter, 10in face
Front wheel size	28in diameter, 6in face
Rear wheel tread	54in
Wheelbase	76in
Turning radius	13ft
Drawbar adjustment	Vertical adjustment: 12, 14, or 16in
	Horizontal adjustment: 26¹⁄₂in
Power takeoff speed	544rpm
Dimensions	Overall width: 64¹⁄₈in
	Overall length: 124in
	Height to radiator cap: 55in
Shipping weight	4,010lb

Source: Deere publication *Power Farming with Greater Profit*, 1937.

Specifications: John Deere Model AR Tractor

Horsepower	All-fuel economy engine: Maximum 30.94hp on the belt, 27.13hp on the drawbar
	Increased-compression gasoline engine: Maximum 39.10hp on the belt, 34.88hp on the drawbar
Speeds	13-26 tires: first, 1¹⁄₃mph; second, 2¹⁄₂mph; third, 3¹⁄₄mph; fourth, 4¹⁄₂mph; fifth, 6¹⁄₄mph; sixth, 11mph; reverse, 2³⁄₄mph
Belt pulley	12³⁄₄in diameter, 7³⁄₈in face, 975rpm
Belt speed	3,270fpm
Power takeoff speed	536rpm; conforms to ASAE standards
Engine	Horizontal two-cylinder, cast-in-block, valves-in-head
	Speed: 975rpm
	Bore and stroke: 5¹⁄₂x6³⁄₄in
	Main bearings: Two steel-backed, Babbitt-lined, removable, 2³⁄₄in diameter, 3¹⁄₄in length
	Connecting rod bearings: Babbitt, centrifugally spun in rod, 3in diameter, 2³⁄₈in width
	Governor: John Deere design, enclosed fly-ball type
	Carburetor: Natural-draft type with load and idle adjustment
	Ignition: High-tension magneto with enclosed automatic impulse starter
	Air cleaner: Oil-wash type with vertical air stack
	Cooling: Tubular radiator, thermo-syphon
	Lubrication: Full force-feed pressure system with oil filter
Starting and lighting	Twelve-volt system with voltage regulator; two front lights and combination rear light and red warning lamp
Fuel tank capacity	All fuel engine: 20 gallons, plus 1 gallon gasoline
	Gasoline engine: 20 gallons
Water capacity	8³⁄₄ gallons
Clutch	Hand-operated, four 10in dry disks, locking in or out
Rear axles	2³⁄₄in diameter; mounted on four tapered roller bearings

Specifications: John Deere Model AR Tractor

Rear tires	Cast wheels: 13-26, 14-26, 14-26 low-profile, and 15-26 cane and rice—all six-ply
Front tires and wheels	6.00x16in four-ply, 7.50x16in six-ply, and 7.50x18in six-ply; disk wheels reversible
Rear wheel tread	54$^7/_{16}$in
Wheelbase	75$^3/_4$in
Turning radius	8ft (approximately, with brakes)
Drawbar adjustments	Conform to ASAE standards for drawbar hitch locations
Dimensions	Overall width: 71$^1/_2$in
	Overall length: 125$^1/_2$in
	Height to radiator cap: 57in
Shipping weight	5,425lb

Source: Deere Publication A-768-51-12 of 1951.

Specifications: John Deere Model AW Tractor

Horsepower	Drawbar load of six-horse team
Speeds	First, 2$^1/_3$mph; second, 3mph; third, 4$^3/_4$mph; fourth, 6$^1/_4$mph; reverse, 3$^1/_2$mph
Belt pulley	3,270fpm
Engine	Two cylinders, cast-in-block, valves-in-head
	Speed: 975rpm
	Bore and stroke: 5$^1/_2$x6$^1/_2$in
	Governor: Enclosed fly-ball type
	Carburetor: Natural-draft type with load and idle adjustment
	Ignition: High-tension magneto with enclosed automatic impulse starter
	Air cleaner: Oil-wash type with vertical air stack
	Lubrication: Full force-feed pressure system with oil filter
	Cooling: Thermo-siphon with gear- and shaft-driven fan
Fuel tank capacity	Fuel: 14 gallons
	Gasoline: 1 gallon
Water capacity	8 gallons
Clutch	Two 10in dry disks, locking in and out
Transmission	Selective spur gear
Rear wheel size	50in diameter, 6in face
Front wheel size	24in diameter, 4in face
Rear wheel tread	Adjustable 56 to 84in
Wheelbase	93$^3/_4$in
Turning radius	16ft, 5$^1/_2$in
Drawbar adjustment	Vertical adjustment: 8 to 15in
	Horizontal adjustment: 26$^1/_2$in
	Lengthwise adjustment: 8$^1/_2$in
Power takeoff speed	544rpm
Dimensions	Overall width: 86in
	Overall length: 136$^1/_4$in
	Height to radiator cap: 61$^1/_2$in
Shipping weight	3,997lb

Source: Deere publication *Power Farming with Greater Profit*, 1937.

Specifications: John Deere Model AO Tractor

Horsepower	Drawbar load of six-horse team; one 22in competitive, or 24in John Deere thresher
Speeds	First, 2mph; second, 3mph; third, 4mph; fourth, 6$^1/_4$mph; reverse, 3mph

Specifications: John Deere Model AO Tractor

Belt pulley	12³⁄₄in diameter, 7¹⁄₂in face, 975rpm; one roller and one bronze bearing
Belt speed	3,270fpm
Engine	Two cylinders, cast-in-block, valves-in-head
	Speed: 975rpm
	Bore and stroke: 5¹⁄₂x6¹⁄₂in
	Crankshaft: Special-quality steel, drop-forged, 3in stock
	Main bearings: Two bronze-backed, Babbitt-lined, removable, 2³⁄₄in diameter, 3¹⁄₄in length
	Connecting rods: Special-quality steel, drop-forged; bearings bronze-backed, 3in diameter, 2³⁄₈in length with bronze bushing for piston pin
	Governor: John Deere design, enclosed fly-ball type with one ball thrust and two self-adjusting ball bearings
	Carburetor: Natural-draft type with dual adjustment
	Ignition: High-tension magneto with enclosed automatic impulse starter
	Air cleaner: Oil wash-down type
	Lubrication: Full force-feed pressure system with oil filter and pressure regulating valve
	Cooling: Thermo-siphon with gear- and shaft-driven fan (no belts or water pump)
Fuel tank capacity	Fuel: 16 gallons
	Gasoline: 1 gallon
Water capacity	8 gallons
Clutch	Two 10in dry disks, locking in and out
Transmission	Selective-type, spur gears, forged, cut, and heat-treated; shafts operating on three taper roller, two taper roller, seven ball, two bronze bearings
Rear axles	2³⁄₄in diameter; mounted on four taper roller bearings
Rear wheel size	42³⁄₄x10in
Front wheel size	28x6in; mounted on four taper roller bearings
Rear wheel tread	51in
Wheelbase	76in
Turning radius	13ft
Turning radius with differential brakes	9ft, 10¹⁄₂in
Drawbar adjustment	Vertical adjustment: 12, 14, or 16in
	Horizontal adjustment: 26¹⁄₂in
Power takeoff speed	544rpm
Dimensions	Overall width: 61in
	Overall length: 124in
	Height to radiator cap: 55in
Shipping weight	4,088lb

Source: Deere Publication Series A240 of 1935.

Specifications: John Deere Model AO Streamlined Grove and Orchard Tractor

Horsepower	Drawbar load of six-horse team; one 24in John Deere thresher, or 22in competitive thresher
Speeds	First, 2mph; second, 3mph; third, 4mph; fourth, 6¹⁄₄mph; reverse, 3mph
Belt pulley	12³⁄₄in diameter, 6¹⁄₄in face, 975rpm; one roller and one bronze bearing
Belt speed	3,270fpm
Engine	Two cylinders, cast-in-block, valves-in-head
	Speed: 975rpm

Specifications: John Deere Model AO Streamlined Grove and Orchard Tractor

	Bore and stroke: $5\frac{1}{2}$x$6\frac{1}{2}$in
	Crankshaft: Special-quality alloy iron, 3in crank pin
	Main bearings: Two bronze-backed, Babbitt-lined, removable; left-hand $2\frac{3}{4}$in diameter, $3\frac{1}{4}$in width; right-hand $3\frac{1}{4}$in diameter, $2\frac{3}{4}$in width
	Connecting rods: Special-quality steel, drop-forged; Babbitt bearings centrifugally spun in rod, 3in diameter, $2\frac{3}{8}$in width
	Governor: John Deere design, enclosed fly-ball type with one ball thrust and two self-adjusting ball bearings
	Carburetor: Natural-draft type with load and idle adjustment
	Ignition: Flange-mounted high-tension magneto with enclosed automatic impulse starter
	Air cleaner: Oil-wash type
	Lubrication: Full force-feed pressure system with oil filter
	Cooling: Thermo-siphon with gear- and shaft-driven fan (no belts or water pump)
Fuel tank capacity	Fuel: 14 gallons
	Gasoline: 1 gallon
Water capacity	7 gallons
Clutch	Two 10in dry disks, locking in and out
Transmission	Selective-type, spur gears, forged, cut, and heat-treated; shafts operating on three taper roller, two taper roller, seven ball bearings
Rear axles	$2\frac{3}{4}$in diameter; mounted on four taper roller bearings
Rear wheel size	$42\frac{3}{4}$x10in
Front wheel size	28x6in; mounted on four taper roller bearings
Rear wheel tread	$45\frac{1}{4}$in
Wheelbase	$69\frac{1}{2}$in
Turning radius	13ft, 4in
Turning radius with differential brakes	9ft
Drawbar adjustment	Vertical adjustment: $11\frac{1}{2}$ to $15\frac{3}{4}$in
	Horizontal adjustment: 30in
Power takeoff speed	544rpm
Dimensions	Overall width: $55\frac{3}{4}$in
	Overall length: $124\frac{1}{4}$in
	Height to radiator cap: $52\frac{1}{4}$in
Shipping weight	4,093lb

Source: Deere Publication Series A344 of 1936.

Specifications: John Deere Model AN Tractor

Horsepower	Drawbar load of six-horse team
Speeds	First, $2\frac{1}{3}$mph; second, 3mph; third, $4\frac{3}{4}$mph; fourth, $6\frac{1}{4}$mph; reverse, $3\frac{1}{2}$mph
Belt pulley	$12\frac{3}{4}$in diameter, $7\frac{1}{4}$in face, 975rpm
Belt speed	3,270fpm
Engine	Two cylinders, cast-in-block, valves-in-head
	Speed: 975rpm
	Bore and stroke: $5\frac{1}{2}$x$6\frac{1}{2}$in
	Governor: Enclosed fly-ball type
	Carburetor: Natural-draft type with load and idle adjustment
	Ignition: High-tension magneto
	Air cleaner: Oil-wash type
	Lubrication: Full force-feed pressure system with oil filter

Specifications: John Deere Model AN Tractor

Engine	Cooling: Thermo-siphon with gear- and shaft-driven fan (no belts or water pump)
Fuel tank capacity	Fuel: 14 gallons
	Gasoline: 1 gallon
Water capacity	8 gallons
Clutch	Two 10in dry disks, locking in and out
Transmission	Selective spur gear
Rear wheel size	50in diameter, 6in face
Front wheel size	24in diameter, 4in face
Rear wheel tread	Adjustable 56 to 84in
Wheelbase	87$\frac{1}{4}$in
Turning radius	8ft
Drawbar adjustment	Vertical adjustment: 8 to 15in
	Horizontal adjustment: 26$\frac{1}{2}$in
	Lengthwise adjustment: 8$\frac{1}{2}$in
Power takeoff speed	544rpm
Dimensions	Overall width: 86in
	Overall length: 130in
	Height to radiator cap: 61$\frac{1}{2}$in
Shipping weight	3,697lb

Source: Deere publication *Power Farming with Greater Profit,* 1937.

Chapter 6

John Deere Model B

Despite the Depression and the collapse of the farm equipment market, the number of tractors on US farms increased by 22 percent between April 1, 1930, and January 1, 1935.

A report issued in 1935 by the Research Department of the Farm Equipment Institute explained the continued growth in farm tractor use: "During the period when prices of farm products were at a low ebb, there naturally was a curtailment in tractor buying. Feed prices were extremely low, and farmers found the cost of horse power materially reduced. With an upturn in prices of grain and hay, however, there was an automatic increase in the cost of horse feed, and tractor power with its other advantages again became much cheaper than animal power. Naturally this resulted in more tractor buying.

"To illustrate the effect of higher prices for farm products on the cost of animal power, it might be cited that the annual cost of feeding one horse, based on average farm prices as of February 15 of each year, was $21.80 in 1933, $48.46 in 1934, and $83.81 in 1935. [Whereas,] the cost of operating a tractor in 1935 is approximately the same as it was in 1932 and 1933."

The study reported that, between 1919 and 1935, the numbers of horses and mules on US farms had been reduced from 26 to 16 million. The report stated, "It is probable that there are not enough good work animals in the United States to provide a team for each farm."

Horsepower is the farmer's most essential requirement. With animal power in limited supply and because mechanical power was more efficient, economical, and satisfactory, it was inevitable that there would continue to be an upward trend in the number of tractors on farms. As illustrated in the chart, tractor sales recovered quickly as the US farm economy strengthened throughout the 1930s.

The One-Plow Tractor

The advent of the one-plow, general-purpose tractor was another significant reason for the continued growth in tractor use and sales.

In the 1930s, there were an estimated 2,000,000 farms with acreage too small to justify investment in a tractor as large as the Deere Model A. Of the estimated 6,288,648 US farms, 37.5 percent, or approximately 2,360,000 farms, were smaller than fifty acres. In fact, in 1930, 59.4 percent of all farms were smaller than 100 acres.

While farms under 100 acres constituted only 15.7 percent of all land under tillage, in number they represented a significant potential market to tractor manufacturers. Large or small, all farmers demanded their own source of horsepower!

To answer the needs of the smaller farmer, International Harvester introduced the Farmall Model F-12 in October 1932. Its four-cylinder engine was rated at 16.20 belt hp and 12.31 drawbar hp, fully capable of pulling one 16in bottom plow.

From its debut, the Farmall F-12 proved extremely popular. In 1937 alone, more than 35,000 units were sold. Introduced with a full line of matched implements and attachments and choice of rubber tires or steel wheels, the F-12 base price of $607 was 30 percent less than that of a two-plow, row-crop tractor.

Deere and Company was also aware of the need for a smaller general-purpose tractor suited to meet the needs of the majority of farmers. So at the same time Deere decided to build the Model A, production plans were also approved for a smaller companion. This tractor became the Model B.

Introduction of the Model B

In almost every respect, the Model B was simply a smaller version of the Model A. Company sales literature promoted the tractor as "approximately two-thirds the size of the Model 'A' in power and weight, but with all of its 'advanced' features." Full-scale production of the B Series began at Waterloo in October 1934 and ended in June 1952.

Like the A Series, the B Series was available in a variety of configurations. At introduction, it shared most of the Model A's distinctive features, which included adjustable rear wheel tread; ample clearance; excellent forward vision for cultivation;

Early Model B with short frame fitted with skeleton rear wheels and self-cleaning front wheels. Its narrow, tapered hood permitted an excellent forward view. Shown *here planting cotton with B37 bedder and planter in Alvarado, Texas.* Deere Archives

hand-clutch four-forward-speed transmission; and a standard centerline hitch and power takeoff. The hydraulic power-lift option and a variety of mounted implements and attachments were also available.

Model B, serial number B 1000 was the first production unit.

The B Series was redesigned by Henry Dreyfuss in 1938. A later restyling followed in 1946. Consequently, as mentioned earlier, models built from 1935 to 1938 are referred to as unstyled, updated tractors built between 1939 and 1946 are referred to as styled, and those that were restyled after World War II are referred to as late-styled.

While estimates of total production vary, the B Series models outsold the A Series and are considered to have been the most popular of all John Deere tractors.

Experimental Model HX

The experimental Model HX first appeared in 1933, a year following the first Model A prototypes. The tractor was tested extensively at facilities in

Tractor Production 1935–1939

Year	Production
1935	161,131
1936	227,185
1937	283,155
1938	199,223
1939	215,462

Source: Agricultural Statistics, 1952, US Department of Commerce.

Arizona's Salt River Valley, and in June 1934 the company issued a formal decision to build the new tractor. Designated the Model B, its production commenced on October 2, 1934, at serial number 1000.

Overview of the Model B

From day one, the Model B was targeted at two segments of the agricultural market. Company officials wrote, "To meet the needs of small farms where the total power requirement does not warrant an outlay as great as the cost of the Model 'A' tractor, and of large farms where a larger tractor is already in operation, and there is a need of a smaller tractor to move quickly and economically, perform the many jobs requiring less power, we will authorize the production of a lighter and less powerful general purpose tractor, designated as the Model 'B.'"

Model B serial number B 1000 is now part of the Keller family collection.

Model B with cultivator; May 1937. Deere Archives

Early Model B generated 14.3 belt hp. In this photo, the tractor powers a Model 5 sheller; January 1936. Deere Archives

While some farmers were undoubtedly looking for a second or third tractor, in 1935 fewer than 15 percent of all US farms employed even one tractor. It was the first-time tractor buyer to whom the Model B most appealed.

The Model B was produced in short-frame and long-frame versions with four- and six-speed transmissions and with distillate-burning (all-fuel) and gasoline-burning engines.

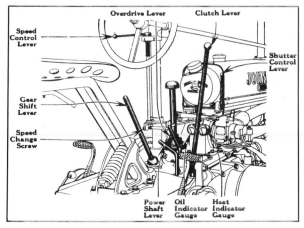

Controls of the four-speed Model B.

Through the course of its production, eight distinct configurations were offered for agricultural applications:

● The two-wheel, tricycle-front Model B
● The single-front-wheel Model BN
● The wide-front Model BW
● The standard-front Model BR
● The orchard version Model BO
● The high-crop version of the Model BN, the BNH
● The high-crop version of the Model BW, the BWH
● The crawler version of the BO, converted by Lindeman Power and Equipment, the Model BO Lindeman.

In addition, narrow versions of the BW and BWH, the BW-40 and BWH-40 respectively, were offered.

A ninth configuration was manufactured, the industrial Model BI. Its history is not a part of this book, however.

B Series Engine

Deere and Company engineering records aptly describe the engine fitted to the B Series at introduction: "The design follows our successfully established practice of two-cylinder construction with ability to satisfactorily burn low cost fuels, thermo-siphon cooling, and pressure lubrication to all bearings. The engine is 4¼inch bore by 5¼inch stroke, valve in head, operating at 1150rpm, and delivering an operating maximum of 16 brake horsepower with fuel consumption less than 0.70 pounds, per brake horsepower hour."

As with the engine fitted to all Deere tractors of the era, the B Series engine was a horizontal design, mounted crosswise on the tractor frame. Its flywheel was on the left-hand side of the tractor.

Spark was generated by a Fairbanks-Morse Model DRV-2B magneto. The carburetor was a Wheeler-Schebler Model DLTX-10 with a 1⅛in throat and flat-type choke lever.

Air intake was via a stack fitted through the hood on the left-hand side of the engine, with exhaust via a stack fitted through the hood on the opposite side. A low air intake stack and low muffler assembly were available as options and were fitted as standard equipment on the Model BR. At introduction, the engine was fitted with a Donaldson oil-washed wire filter air cleaner.

The engine was fitted with a centrifugal-type governor of Deere's own manufacture, and set to maintain engine speed at 1150rpm under load and 1310rpm at idle.

In its official Nebraska test of November 15, 1934, to April 19, 1935 (Official Tractor Test No. 232), the engine generated 14.30hp at the belt pulley and 9.38hp at the drawbar, operating under rated load.

A Larger Engine

In 1939, Deere introduced a new engine, with bore and stroke of 4½x5½in. Tested at Nebraska between September 6 and September 16, 1938 (Official Tractor Test No. 305), it was rated at 16.86 engine hp and 10.76 drawbar hp. In comparison to the earlier engine, it delivered 15 percent more horsepower at the drawbar.

Other changes to the engine at that time included a change of magneto to a Wico Model C-1042, and a Motor Improvements, Incorporated full-flow engine oil filter with by-pass, which used an impregnated, replaceable paper element.

Further Testing at Nebraska

Three more official tests of the Model B were carried out at Nebraska. Between November 7, 1940, and April 25, 1941 (Official Tractor Test No. 366), a six-speed version of the Model B was tested.

With a change in carburetor to a Schebler DLTX-34 with 1½in throat, the tractor was rated at 17.46hp at the belt and 14.08hp at the drawbar, an increase of 31 percent.

In 1947, the company increased the bore of the B Series engine to 4¹¹⁄₁₆in and offered both an all-fuel version and a higher compression gasoline engine. The gasoline version was tested in Lincoln between April 28 and May 14, 1947 (Official Tractor Test No. 380). The new engine was rated at 24.39 belt hp and 19.13 drawbar hp, a further increase of

Model B with rubber in front and skeleton steel in rear. At introduction, steel wheels with lugs were standard. Photographed with Model 614 baler. Deere Archives

Rubber tires fitted to spoke wheels. Deere Archives

40 percent at the pulley and 36 percent at the drawbar.

The all-fuel version was tested in Lincoln between May 9 and May 15, 1947 (Official Tractor Test No. 381), and rated at 20.68 belt hp and 16.64 drawbar hp.

The Model B was fitted with a belt pulley with 10⅝in diameter and 6in face. It rotated at 1150rpm and was rated at 3,200fpm.

Longer Frame

Perhaps the most noticeable change or modification to the Model B was the lengthening of its frame, or front support. In June 1937, beginning

with serial number 42200, 5in was added to the frame. This modification permitted an interchangeability of integral (mounted) implements with the larger Model A.

The longer frame necessitated a number of other changes which, according to *Two-Cylinder*, included hood, fuel tank, radiator shutter control rod, upper water pipe, lower water pipe, fan shaft, fan shaft tube, steering rod, crankcase ventilator pipe, and carburetor intake elbow.

Transmission and Final Drives

The transmission fitted to the unstyled Model B featured four forward speeds and one reverse

Rubber tires fitted to cast wheels on styled Model B tractor and Model F Van Brunt grain drill. Deere Archives

speed: first, 2¹/₃mph; second, 3mph; third, 4mph; fourth, 5mph; and reverse, 3¹/₂mph.

In 1941, the six-speed transmission was fitted to the 4¹/₂x5¹/₂in engine introduced in 1939. Advertised speeds were as follows: first, 2¹/₃mph; second, 3¹/₄mph; third, 4mph; fourth, 5¹/₃mph; fifth, 7¹/₄mph; sixth, 12¹/₄mph; and reverse, 4mph.

As with the six-speed transmission of the Model A, the unit employed a dual-shift (two-lever) system with a "Hi" and "Lo" range, and an all-spur-gear final drive rather than sprockets and roller chain.

Wheels and Tires

At introduction, the standard drive wheels fitted to the Model B were 48x5¹/₄in steel wheels with 4¹/₄in lugs. Front steel wheels were 22x3¹/₄in.

Optional rear tire sizes included 7.50x36in four-ply; 7.50x36in six-ply; 9.00x36in four-ply; 9.00x36in six-ply; 7.50x40in four-ply; and 9.00x40in six-ply, all mounted on steel-spoke

With rear wheels set to the narrowest width and the added benefit of an inline hitch, the plow trailed within the wheel tread. Deere Archives

Notice the PTO shaft and late-styled hitch on this tractor, whose wheels are set for planting cotton with a B-253

Cotton and Corn Planter. Also note the chain drive off the rear wheel sprocket; May 1939. Deere Archives

Left rear wheel is offset on this unit with trailing mower and windrower; August 1939. Deere Archives

Model B had more than enough power to handle B241 middlebreaker with two 125 bottoms. Deere Archives

Model B with potato planter. Photographed on Rockefeller Farm, Phelps, New York, June 1939. Deere Archives

wheels. A cast rear wheel was offered with 7.50x36in four- and six-ply, or 9.00x36in four- and six-ply tires.

Adjustable Rear Wheel Tread

The B Series rear tread width varied by model. For the standard Model B, tread width was adjustable between 56 and 84in; for the BNH and BWH models, tread width was adjustable between 56 and 104in. The narrow-rear-end versions of the BW, BW-40, and BWH-40 offered rear wheel tread

that ranged between 40 and 72in, depending upon wheel and tire equipment. The Model BR rear tread width was fixed at 68in, as were those of the orchard Model BO and the industrial Model BI.

Drawbar Performance

While the company promoted the Model B as having had two-thirds the capacity of the Model A, a comparison of Nebraska test results reveals that the drawbar pull of the Model B was, in fact, only 55 percent of that of the Model A.

Integral cultivator mounted to Model B. Before herbicides were introduced, corn was often grown in "checked" rows to permit cultivation both lengthwise and crosswise. Deere Archives

Model B with corn binder. Deere Archives

However, with a drawbar pull of 1,728lb under maximum load, the Model B supplied ample power to match "the daily work output of six to eight horses." According to a 1937 sales brochure, a drawbar would accomplish ten different tasks: plow up to seven acres in a ten-hour day; single-disk thirty-five to forty acres with a 10ft disk harrow; list or bed eight to twelve acres; plant twenty to twenty-five acres a day with a two-row planter; drill twenty to thirty acres; cultivate from twenty-five to forty acres in a ten-hour day; cut twenty-five to thirty-five acres of hay with a power mower; harvest twenty-five to forty acres a day with an 8ft binder; pull a one-row potato digger; and furnish steady, ample power on drawbar, belt, and power takeoff for many other farm jobs within its power range.

The extension of the Model B's front support frame permitted Deere to offer buyers the full array of integral implements suited to the Model A, but with a more limited size range. For example, while two- and four-row cultivators were available and could be fitted to the Model A, it was the two-row version that was suited to the Model B.

As a guideline, the Model B was rated to pull one 16in bottom plow, a one-bottom middlebreaker, a two-row planter, or a two-row cultivator.

Model B Modifications

The Models B, BN, BW, BNH, and BWH were styled in 1938 by Henry Dreyfuss; the BR, BO, and BI versions were never styled.

The unstyled B Series underwent a number of modifications among which included, according to *Two-Cylinder*, a lengthened rear axle, at serial number 11505; change in crankcase cover, at serial number 10169; change in the drawbar end, from a loop-type to an end suited to a standard drawbar pin, at serial number 42200; optional fenders from those with a sharp 90 degree side with single raised rib on the outer top part of the fender, to a contoured, smooth-top surface with a slightly rounded outer edge, in 1937; change in flywheel casting; change in fuel tank, from that with filler opening in the top center to one with filler cocked to the left (the steering rod interfered with the

Model B fitted with loader and pulling H & B spreader. Deere Archives

Model B tractor and Model 11 combine; May 1939. Deere
Archives

original opening); installation of a heat indicator
gauge, starting with serial number 12743; and two
changes in the hood—the first when the fuel tanks
were changed, at serial number 1510, and the
second when the frame was lengthened by 5in, at
serial number 42200.

The styled Model B was modified in the same
fashion and was offered with many of the same
option packages, as was the styled Model A. These
included optional electric starting and lighting in
1940 (electric start and lights became standard in
1947); the Roll-O-Matic front end; Powr-Trol re-

Model B fitted with Dain push rake; July 1939. Deere
Archives

*Styled Model B. Grille on Model B had seven louvers,
while Model A had eight.* Deere Archives

Lights and electric starting were optional before 1947.
Deere Archives

mote hydraulics in 1945; a cushioned operator seat
with backrest in 1947; single shift lever; welded
steel frame; enclosed flywheel; and an optional
split- or two-piece front pedestal, which permitted
interchangeable front ends—dual front, dual front
with Roll-O-Matic, adjustable front, and single
front wheel for narrow-space rows, all in 1947.

Model BN Narrow-Front

The Model BN was introduced in 1935 and
remained in production until May 1952. It featured
a single front wheel. Designed specifically for use
by market gardeners, truck farmers, or market
growers, the tractor was initially referred to as the
B Garden Tractor.

Company records indicate the unit was built
"to provide a Model 'B' tractor which [was] better
adapted to the cultivation of beets, lettuce and
other vegetables which [were] planted in rows of 28
inches or less."

The standard steel rear wheels were the same
as those offered on the Model B, 48in diameter by

5¼in face. Rubber tires were optional. The unit was equipped with a single front wheel 22½x8in, supported by a yoke. Single or double rubber tires were available.

The changes in mounting necessitated a different pedestal and front-end assembly than were fitted to the Model B. Early units were built with a welded steel frame and a pedestal bolted to the frame with four bolts. A cast-iron frame was substituted at serial number 3943, and an eight-bolt pedestal was fitted.

Model BW Wide-Front

In February 1935, Deere introduced the Model BW as a counterpart to the narrow-front Model BN. It remained in production until June 1952.

The BW featured a pivoting front end, adjustable between 56 and 80in in four-inch steps. By moving out one side at a time, 2in intervals could also be secured.

According to engineering records, its purpose was "to provide an adjustable-tread front axle for the Model 'B' tractor to which standard tillage tools

In 1947, the flywheel on the A and B models was enclosed. Standard electric starting meant flywheel no longer had to be turned over by hand to start tractor. Deere Archives

Welded steel frame, cushioned seat with backrest, and "B" decal on side indicate circa 1947. Deere Archives

[might] be attached and to reduce packing of the soil."

With the front and rear axles set at the same tread width, the Model BW offered the same advantages as a standard-tread tractor, which included front and rear wheels that could track in all tread positions; improved longitudinal and lateral stability; greater lateral holding power of guide bands in soil due to increased spacing; less intensive soil packing; and easier steering when plowing. (Either front wheel could ride in the furrow. When production of the standard-tread BR ceased in January 1947, the fact that the BW's front end could be set to the same width as its rear tread made it a suitable substitute.)

In February 1937, Deere made the decision to build a "special narrow" version of the BW. Designated the BW-40, the tractor featured adjustable front tread of 40 to 52in and offered an adjustable rear tread width between 40 and 72in.

The tractor was targeted for use in row-crops spaced as small as 20in. Components from the Model BR were used to "reduce the width of the tractor through the pulley and flywheel" and "to give more clearance for the reduced rear-wheel tread." Further, the rear axle housing and rear axles were also replaced.

While the company forecasted an annual production of 150 units, only 6 were manufactured. Consequently, the company canceled the project and in its place elected to build a high-crop version, designated the Model BWH-40.

Model BR Standard-Tread

As stated, the Model D was rated as a three-plow standard tractor. The Model AR was introduced in April 1935 as a two-plow standard unit, and the BR one-plow standard tractor followed in September 1935.

While it is difficult to imagine the need for a one-plow standard tractor, particularly when the company offered the more versatile BW, Deere promoted the tractor as it did the other two standard machines.

In sales literature, the Model BR was advertised as a "new standard of value in standard tread tractors . . . able to handle the loads ordinarily

Wide-front BW featured adjustable front end between 56 and 80in; June 1936. Deere Archives

pulled by . . . a four-horse team." Its strengths at the drawbar, in transport work and in belt pulley operations, were cited as making the BR an "outstanding value."

Interestingly, the company advertised the BR as "built low down to make an ideal tractor for orchard as well as field and belt jobs." That was a pragmatic declaration, as the standard and orchard tractors were almost identical in overall dimensions.

Built only in an unstyled version, production of the Model BR was suspended in January 1947.

Model BO Orchard Tractor

The grove and orchard version of the Model B, the Model BO, was introduced at the same time as the BR, and offered all the benefits of the larger Model AO.

Available with steel wheels or rubber tires mounted on cast wheels and optional citrus fenders, the BO was a popular, lower-priced alternative to the AO. Standing 50in wide and 52in tall, the BO was a compact unit that met the needs of smaller grove, orchard, and vineyard operations.

Like the Model BR, the BO was never restyled. Its production was also suspended in January 1947.

Model BO Lindeman: A Crawler Tractor for the West

While not built by Deere, the Model BO Lindeman crawler tractor was a favorite among growers on western hillsides, and it remains a favorite among collectors today.

Between 1939 and 1947, some 2,000 Model BO units were shipped to Lindeman Power and Equipment in Yakima, Washington, for conversion to

Two-row potato hoe mounted to BW; August 1935. Deere Archives

Beginning in 1939, Lindeman Power and Equipment of Yakima, Washington, purchased orchard versions of the

Model B (Model BO) and fitted them with crawler tracks for use in Pacific Northwest orchards. Deere Archives

track machines. It was the Lindeman BO that led Deere and Company into the manufacture of crawler tractors. In 1946, Deere purchased Lindeman with the intention of building a new track machine.

The new machine, the Model MC, was based on the Model M tractor introduced by Deere in 1947. The MC was built partially in Yakima and partially in Dubuque, Iowa. Eventually, however, the company opted to transfer all assembly work to Dubuque.

Models BNH and BWH High-Crop Tractors

In August 1937, the company decided to build a high-crop version of the Model BN. In October 1937, they added the high-crop version of the Model BW to their current line.

The BNH and BWH were hybrids built from components taken from the Models B, BN, and BW, as well as newly designed components unique to these models.

The Model BNH provided an additional 2in clearance at the rear, which resulted from the use of 7.50x40in rubber-tired drive wheels instead of 7.50x36in tires (no steel-wheel option); an added 4¼in clearance at the front, which resulted from an increase in rubber-tired front wheel from 7.50x10 to 6.50x16in; a rear tread adjustment from 56 to 104in, achieved by an increase in width over axles from 85⅝ to 97½in; and a change of rear axle housing, which allowed an additional 2⅞in length to each arm and an increased diameter of ⅛in.

Model BNH offered a high-clearance, narrow configuration for use in tall vegetable farming.

LOS FAMOSOS TRACTORES "JOHN DEERE" PARA GASOIL

TRACTOR MODELO "D"

El tractor mas grande que fabrica "John Deere". Únicamente de tipo de cuatro ruedas, para trabajo pesado con implementos de arrastre. Tiene tres velocidades hacia adelante.

TRACTOR MODELO "G"

El tractor mas grande para trabajar con implementos de arrastre y con implementos montados sobre el tractor. Tiene las ruedas traseras ajustables y las delanteras juntas. Cuatro velocidades hacia adelante.

TRACTOR MODELO "A"

El tractor mediano para toda clase de trabajo, cultiva y siembra hasta cuatro surcos y arrastra un arado de tres discos. Tiene las ruedas traseras ajustables y las delanteras juntas. Cuatro velocidades hacia adelante.

TRACTOR MODELO "B"

El tractor chico para toda clase de trabajo, cultiva y siembra dos surcos y arrastra un arado de dos discos. Tiene las ruedas traseras ajustables y las delanteras juntas. Cuatro velocidades hacia adelante.

TRACTOR MODELO "AR"

Este es el tractor mediano para implementos de arrastre, como el Modelo "A", trabaja con arado de tres discos y otros implementos que piden la misma fuerza. Este tractor difere del Modelo "A" únicamente en que es del tipo de cuatro ruedas.

TRACTOR MODELO "BR"

Este tractor es de la potencia del Modelo "B", tiene la fuerza para un arado de dos discos o para cualquier otro implemento que pide la misma fuerza. Es del tipo de cuatro ruedas para trabajar únicamente con implementos de arrastre.

TRACTOR MODELO "AO"

Este tractor es como el Modelo "AR", es de tipo de cuatro ruedas pero está hecho mas bajo y tiene las ruedas y el mecanismo bien cubierto para que puede trabajar en huertas sin lastimar los árboles.

TRACTOR MODELO "BO"

Este es el tractor chico para trabajar en huertas. Es del tipo y potencia del Modelo "BR" pero mas bajo y protegido para que no puede lastimar los árboles frutales.

TRACTORES MODELO "AW" y "BW"

Los dos tamaños de los tractores "A" y "B" se puede suministrar con las ruedas delanteras y traseras ajustables desde 142 hasta 203 cms. Estos tractores trabajan con implementos montados y tambien de arrastre, tienen muchas ventajas en tierras atascosas.

(VUELTA)

A399—38-9

Models A and B dominated this 1938 Spanish-language export ad. Deere Archives

All BNH units were built on the longer frame and were restyled in 1938. Production began in October 1937 and was suspended in December 1946.

According to engineering records, the Model BWH was introduced to "meet a wider variety of field requirements in raising vegetable crops where it is desired to operate with one row under the center of the tractor."

An additional 2in of clearance was provided under the rear axle through use of the same wheels and tires fitted to the BNH. Three inches of additional clearance at the front were achieved through use of lengthened front axle knuckles.

Standard front wheel tread adjustment was from $42^{5}/_{8}$ to $54^{5}/_{8}$in, versus 40 to 52in on the Model BW. Both 7 and 13in extension assemblies were available that offered front wheel tread adjust-

ments of $56^{5}/_{8}$ to $68^{5}/_{8}$in, and $68^{5}/_{8}$ to $80^{5}/_{8}$in, respectively.

The BWH was fitted with the same rear axle as that fitted to the BNH and therefore offered the same 56 to 104in rear wheel tread adjustment.

All BWH units were also built on the longer frame. Production began in December 1937 and was suspended in December 1946.

Soon after the decision was made to build the BWH, the company suspended plans to manufacture the previously approved Model BW-40. In its place, it was decided that a high-crop unit designated the Model BWH-40 would be built.

The BWH-40 offered adjustable rear wheel tread of $42^{1}/_{2}$ to 80in: $42^{1}/_{2}$ to 56in with the wheel rims set in, and $58^{3}/_{4}$ to 80in with the rims set out. Front tread adjustment was the same as that of the regular BWH, $42^{5}/_{8}$ to $80^{5}/_{8}$in, and was attained

Favorites among farmers and collectors: a line-up of Models A and B, ready for delivery; February 1936.
Deere Archives

through the use of the same 7 or 13in extension assemblies. Because the narrowest rear wheel tread setting placed the tires dangerously close to the operator, fenders were furnished as standard equipment.

The number of Model BWH-40 units built is unknown. *Two-Cylinder* estimated the number at no more than twenty tractors.

Farewell to Model B

On June 2, 1952, the last units of Models B and BW were built. Efficient, sturdy machines, the B Series was the best-selling series of tractors in the history of Deere and Company. In July 1952, production began on its successor, the 50 Series.

Although the 50 Series were notable successors, they remained in production for only four years whereas production of the B Series spanned almost two decades.

The Model B has long been the favorite among farmers and collectors alike. Perhaps more than any other Deere tractor model, it established the company as a Goliath among the world's tractor manufacturers.

Specifications: John Deere Model B General Purpose Tractor with Adjustable Tread

Horsepower	Drawbar load of four-horse team
Speeds	First, $2^1/_3$mph; second, 3mph; third, 4mph; fourth, 5mph; reverse, $3^1/_2$mph
Belt pulley	$10^5/_8$in diameter, 6in face, 1150rpm
Belt speed	3,200fpm
Engine	Two cylinders, cast-in-block, valves-in-head
	Speed: 1150rpm
	Bore and stroke: $4^1/_4$x$5^1/_4$in
	Crankshaft: Special-quality steel, drop-forged, $2^1/_2$in crank pins
	Main bearings: Two bronze-backed, Babbitt-lined, removable, $2^1/_4$in diameter, $2^1/_2$in width
	Connecting rods: Special-quality steel, drop-forged; Babbitt bearings centrifugally spun in rod, $2^1/_2$in diameter, 2in width; bronze bushings
	Governor: John Deere design, enclosed fly-ball type with one-ball thrust and two self-adjusting ball bearings
	Carburetor: Natural-draft type with load and idle adjustment
	Ignition: High-tension magneto with enclosed automatic impulse starter
	Air cleaner: Oil-wash type with vertical air stack
	Lubrication: Full force-feed pressure system with oil filter
	Cooling: Thermo-syphon with gear- and shaft-driven fan (no belts or water pump)
Fuel tank capacity	Fuel: $13^1/_2$ gallons
	Gasoline: 1 gallon
Water capacity	$5^1/_2$ gallons
Clutch	8in dry disks, locking in and out
Transmission	Selective-type, spur gears, forged, cut, and heat-treated; shafts operating on three roller, four tapered roller, five ball bearings
Rear axles	$2^3/_8$in diameter; mounted on four tapered roller bearings
Rear wheel size	48in diameter, $3^1/_4$in face; mounted on four tapered roller bearings
Rear wheel tread	56 to 84in
Wheelbase	85in
Turning radius	7ft, 8in
Drawbar adjustment	Vertical adjustment: 9 to 13in
	Horizontal adjustment: 24in
	Lengthwise adjustment: $8^1/_2$in
Power takeoff speed	553rpm
Dimensions	Overall width: 85in
	Overall length: 128in
	Height to radiator cap: 56in
Width	86in
Shipping weight	2,731lb

Source: Deere Publication Series A188 of 1937.

Specifications: John Deere Model B General Purpose Tractor with Adjustable Tread

Horsepower Two 14in plow bottoms or a two-bottom bedder under normal conditions

Speeds First, 2½mph; second, 3¼mph; third, 4¼mph; fourth, 5½mph; fifth, 7⅓mph; sixth, 12½mph; reverse, 4mph

Belt pulley 10⅝in diameter, 6³⁄₁₆in face, 1150rpm; one roller and one bronze bearing

Belt speed 3,200fpm

Engine Two cylinders, cast-in-block; valves-in-head
Speed: 1150rpm
Bore and stroke: 4½x5½in
Crankshaft: Special-quality steel, drop-forged, 2¾in crank pins
Main bearings: Two bronze-backed, Babbitt-lined; removable; right-hand 2¼in diameter, 2⁹⁄₁₆in length; left-hand 2¼in diameter, 2¾in length
Connecting rods: Special-quality steel, drop forged; Babbitt bearings centrifugally spun in rod 2¾in diameter x 2in wide. Bronze bushing for piston pin.
Governor: John Deere design, enclosed fly-ball with one ball thrust and two self-adjusting ball bearings
Carburetor: Natural-draft type with load and idle adjustment
Ignition: High-tension magneto with enclosed automatic impulse starter
Air cleaner: Oil-wash type
Lubrication: Full force-feed pressure system with oil filter
Cooling: Thermo-siphon with gear- and shaft-driven fan (no belts or water pump)

Fuel tank capacity Fuel: 12 gallons
Gasoline: 2 gallons

Water capacity 6¼ gallons

Clutch Two 8in dry disks, locking in and out

Transmission Selective-type, spur gears, forged, cut, and heat-treated; shafts operating on three roller, four tapered, five ball bearings

Rear axles 2½in diameter; mounted on four tapered roller bearings

Rear wheels Tire sizes/wheel equipment:
8-38 four-ply pressed-steel or cast
8-38 six-ply pressed-steel or cast
9-38* four-ply pressed-steel or cast
9-38 six-ply pressed-steel or cast
10-38 four-ply pressed-steel or cast
10-38 six-ply pressed-steel or cast
11-38 four-ply pressed-steel or cast
11-38 six-ply pressed-steel or cast
*Mounted on cast wheels; recommended for average field conditions.
Note: Cast wheels were approximately 265lb heavier than steel wheels.
Steel-spoke wheels with lugs were available as special equipment, diameter 48in, face 5¼in (furnished with four speeds only).

Front wheel size 5.00x15in four-ply rubber tires; mounted on four tapered roller bearings; steel-spoke wheels with guide bands available as special equipment, diameter 22in, face 3¼in

Rear wheel tread 56 to 84in

Wheelbase 85in

Turning radius 7ft, 8in

Drawbar adjustment Vertical adjustment: 11½ to 14¼in
Horizontal adjustment: 24in
Lengthwise adjustment: 11⅛in

Power takeoff speed 564rpm

Dimensions Overall width: 83in
Overall length: 127¼in
Overall height: 78⅛in
Height to radiator cap: 58in

Shipping weight 3,461lb

Note: Dimensions and weight are based on 9-38 four-ply tires mounted on cast wheels.
Source: Deere Publication Series A456 of 1941.

Specifications: John Deere Model B General Purpose Tractor with Adjustable Tread

Horsepower	All-fuel economy engine: Maximum 22.19hp on the drawbar and 24.33 on the belt
	Increased-compression gasoline engine: Maximum 25.50hp on the drawbar and 28.69 on the belt
Speeds	First, 1½mph; second, 2½mph; third, 3½mph; fourth, 4½mph; fifth, 5¾mph; sixth, 10mph; reverse, 2½mph
Belt pulley	Regular equipment, 9¹¹⁄₁₆in diameter, 7¼in face, 1250rpm
Belt speed	3,110fpm
Power takeoff speed	Conforms to ASAE power takeoff standards
Engine	Two cylinders, cast-in-block, valves-in-head
	Speed: 1250rpm
	Bore and stroke: 4¹¹⁄₁₆x5½in
	Main bearings: Two steel-backed, Babbitt-lined, removable; right-hand 2¼in diameter, 2⁹⁄₁₆in width; left-hand 2¼in diameter, 2¾in width
	Connecting rod bearings: Babbitt, centrifugally spun in rod, 2¾in diameter, 2in width
	Governor: John Deere design, enclosed fly-ball with one ball thrust and two self-adjusting ball bearings
	Carburetor: Natural-draft type with load and idle adjustment
	Ignition: High-tension magneto with enclosed automatic impulse starter
	Air cleaner: Oil-wash type
	Lubrication: Full force-feed pressure system with oil filter
	Cooling: Thermo-siphon with gear- and shaft-driven fan (no belts or water pump)
Starting and lighting	Regular equipment, six-volt system with voltage regulator; two front lights and one rear light
Fuel tank capacity	All-fuel engine: 12 gallons, plus 1 gallon gasoline
	Gasoline engine: 14 gallons
Water capacity	6¾ gallons
Clutch	Four 7in dry disks, locking in and out
Rear axles	2½in diameter; mounted on four tapered roller bearings
Rear tires and wheels	10-38 four-ply, on cast- or pressed-steel wheels
Front tires and wheels	5.50x16in four-ply; disk wheels reversible
Rear wheel tread	56 to 88in
Wheelbase	90in
Turning radius	8ft, 7½in
Drawbar adjustments	Conform to ASAE standards for drawbar hitch locations
Dimensions	Overall width: 87in
	Overall length: 132¼in
	Overall height: 79⅞in
	Height to radiator cap: 59⅝in
Shipping weight	4,052lb with power lift and cast rear wheels

Source: Deere Publication Series A56 of 1947.

Specifications: John Deere Model BR Tractor

Horsepower	Drawbar load of four-horse team
Speeds	First, 2mph; second, 3mph; third, 4mph; fourth, 6¼mph; reverse, 3mph
Belt pulley	10⅝in diameter, 5½in face, 1150rpm
Belt speed	3,200fpm
Engine	Two cylinders, cast-in-block, valves-in-head
	Speed: 1150rpm
	Bore and stroke: 4¼x5¼in

Specifications: John Deere Model BR Tractor

Governor: Enclosed fly-ball type
Carburetor: Natural-draft type with load and idle adjustment
Ignition: High-tension magneto
Air cleaner: Oil-wash type
Lubrication: Full force-feed pressure system with oil filter
Cooling: Thermo-siphon with gear- and shaft-driven fan (no belts or water pump)

Fuel tank capacity	Fuel: 12 gallons
	Gasoline: 1 gallon
Water capacity	$5^{1}/_{2}$ gallons
Clutch	Two 8in dry disks, locking in and out
Transmission	Selective spur gear
Rear wheel size	40in diameter, 8in face
Front wheel size	24in diameter, 5in face
Rear wheel tread	$44^{1}/_{4}$in
Wheelbase	68in
Turning radius	11ft, 8in
Drawbar adjustment	Vertical adjustment: 12,14, or 16in
	Horizontal adjustment: $25^{3}/_{4}$in
Power takeoff speed	553rpm
Dimensions	Overall width: $52^{1}/_{4}$in
	Overall length: $117^{3}/_{4}$in.
	Height to radiator cap: $50^{1}/_{2}$in
Shipping weight	2,889lb

Source: Deere publication *Power Farming with Greater Profit*, 1937.

Specifications: John Deere Model BW Tractor

Horsepower	Drawbar load of four-horse team
Speeds	First, $2^{1}/_{3}$mph; second, 3mph; third, $4^{3}/_{4}$mph; fourth, $6^{1}/_{4}$mph; reverse, $3^{1}/_{2}$mph
Belt pulley	$10^{5}/_{8}$in diameter, 6in face, 1150rpm
Belt speed	3,200fpm
Engine	Two cylinders, cast-in-block, valves-in-head
	Speed: 1150rpm
	Bore and stroke: $4^{1}/_{4}$x$5^{1}/_{4}$in
	Governor: Enclosed fly-ball type
	Carburetor: Natural-draft type with load and idle adjustment
	Ignition: High-tension magneto
	Air cleaner: Oil-wash type
	Lubrication: Full force-feed pressure system with oil filter
	Cooling: Thermo-siphon with gear- and shaft-driven fan (no belts or water pump)
Fuel tank capacity	Fuel: 12 gallons
	Gasoline: 1 gallon
Water capacity	$5^{1}/_{2}$ gallons
Clutch	Two 8in dry disks, locking in and out
Transmission	Selective spur gear
Rear wheel size	48in diameter, $5^{1}/_{4}$in face
Front wheel size	24in diameter, 4in face
Rear wheel tread	Adjustable 56 to 84in
Wheelbase	$86^{3}/_{8}$in
Turning radius	15ft, 3in
Drawbar adjustment	Vertical adjustment: 9 to 13in
	Horizontal adjustment: 24in
	Lengthwise adjustment: $8^{1}/_{2}$in

Specifications: John Deere Model BW Tractor

Power takeoff speed	553rpm
Dimensions	Overall width: 85in
	Overall length: 128in
	Height to radiator cap: 56in
Shipping weight	3,051lb

Source: Deere publication *Power Farming with Greater Profit,* 1937.

Specifications: John Deere Model BO Tractor

Horsepower	Drawbar load of four-horse team
Speeds	First, 2mph; second, 3mph; third, 4mph; fourth, 6¼mph; reverse, 3mph
Belt speed	3,200fpm
Engine	Two cylinders, cast-in-block, valves-in-head
	Speed: 1150rpm
	Bore and stroke: 4¼x5¼in
	Governor: Enclosed fly-ball type
	Carburetor: Natural-draft type with load and idle adjustment
	Ignition: High-tension magneto
	Air cleaner: Oil-wash type
	Lubrication: Full force-feed pressure system with oil filter
	Cooling: Thermo-siphon with gear- and shaft-driven fan (no belts or water pump)
Fuel tank capacity	Fuel: 12 gallons
	Gasoline: 1 gallon
Water capacity	5½ gallons
Clutch	Two 8in dry disks, locking in and out
Transmission	Selective spur gear
Rear wheel size	40in diameter, 8in face
Front wheel size	24in diameter, 5in face
Rear wheel tread	41¼in
Wheelbase	68in
Turning radius	11ft, 8in; with differential brakes, 8ft, 8in
Drawbar adjustment	Vertical adjustment: 12, 14, or 16in
	Horizontal adjustment: 25¾in
Power takeoff speed	553rpm
Dimensions	Overall width: 50in
	Overall length: 117¾in
	Height to radiator cap: 50½in
Shipping weight	2,941lb

Source: Deere publication *Power Farming with Greater Profit,* 1937.

Specifications: John Deere Model BN Tractor

Horsepower	Drawbar load of four-horse team
Speeds	First, 2⅓mph; second, 3mph; third, 4¾mph; fourth, 6¼mph; reverse, 3½mph
Belt pulley	10⅝in diameter, 6in face, 1150rpm
Belt speed	3,200fpm
Engine	Two cylinders, cast-in-block, valves-in-head
	Speed: 1150rpm
	Bore and stroke: 4¼x5¼in
	Governor: Enclosed fly-ball type
	Carburetor: Natural-draft type with load and idle adjustment
	Ignition: High-tension magneto
	Air cleaner: Oil-wash type

Specifications: John Deere Model BN Tractor

Engine	Lubrication: Full force-feed pressure system with oil filter
	Cooling: Thermo-siphon with gear- and shaft-driven fan (no belts or water pump)
Fuel tank capacity	Fuel: 12 gallons
	Gasoline: 1 gallon
Water capacity	5$\frac{1}{2}$ gallons
Clutch	Two 8in dry disks, locking in and out
Transmission	Selective spur gear
Front wheel size	22$\frac{1}{2}$in diameter, 8in face
Rear wheel size	48in diameter, 5$\frac{1}{4}$in face
Rear wheel tread	Adjustable 56 to 84in
Wheelbase	80in
Turning radius	8ft
Drawbar adjustment	Vertical adjustment: 9 to 13in
	Horizontal adjustment: 24in
	Lengthwise adjustment: 8$\frac{1}{2}$in
Power takeoff speed	553rpm
Dimensions	Overall width: 85in
	Overall length: 120$\frac{1}{2}$in
	Height to radiator cap: 56in
Shipping weight	2,763lb

Source: Deere publication *Power Farming with Greater Profit,* 1937.

Chapter 7

John Deere Model G

The quarter century between 1928 and 1953 witnessed several trends in US agriculture that are particularly relevant to the story of the tractor. Among these trends were changes in the number and size of farms, and the decline in the farm population. In 1930, the US Bureau of Census recorded 6,288,648 farms. By 1950, that number had declined by 15 percent. Yet, between 1930 and 1950, the amount of land being farmed increased by 21 percent.

In 1930, as many as 29,447,000 Americans lived on farms—24 percent of the total population. By 1951, the farm population had fallen by 6,000,000 to a number that constituted 15.1 percent of the total population, a decline of 37 percent in only two decades. To a large degree, it was the introduction of the affordable, all-purpose tractor that led to these changes.

As farms grew larger, and as the farmhands moved into town, agriculture's demand for mechanical horsepower increased. In 1930, there were 920,000 tractors in use on American farms. By 1940, the number reached 1,545,000, an increase of 68 percent. As illustrated, the robust tractor production of the middle to late 1930s continued between 1940 and 1950.

In 1953, the USDA reported 4,400,000 tractors in use. For the first time, the number of tractors equaled the number of automobiles owned by America's farmers. After thirty-five years, Henry Ford's ambition had been fulfilled. The tractor had become as common a machine on the farm as was the automobile.

As the number of tractors manufactured increased, so did their average horsepower output. Although the late 1930s saw the birth of what were called "baby tractors"—general-purpose tractors with belt horsepower ratings of 10 or less (Deere's Model L is a good example)—the overall demand was for greater horsepower.

Horsepower ratings of the Models A and B were increased dramatically through the years in which they were built. In 1947, the belt horsepower rating of the high-compression Model B was

Tractor Production and Tractors on Farms 1940–1950

Year	Production	Tractors on farms
1940	283,546	1,545,000
1941	358,520	
1942	215,074	
1943	143,489	
1944	310,990	
1945	317,268	2,422,000
1946	402,413	
1947	643,567	
1948	753,623	
1949	726,975	
1950	693,646	3,615,000

Source: Agricultural Statistics, 1952, US Department of Commerce.

greater than that of the Model A at its introduction. And the Model AR easily rivaled the productive capacity of the standard Model D.

As popular a tractor as was the Model A, it could not efficiently meet the requirements of the growing number of large row-crop operations. With that in mind, Deere engineers turned their attention to the development of what became the largest row-crop tractor on the market—the three-plow Model G.

Introduction of the Model G

According to company records, the Model G was introduced "to meet the needs of larger farms [that required] a general purpose tractor [with] greater power at both the belt and the drawbar than that [which was] available from the Model 'A.'"

The Model G supplied three-plow power for any type of field work. As such, it was designed to appeal to small-grain farmers who also grew row-crops, as well as to large corn, cotton, and vegetable growers.

Production of the Model G began in May 1937 and was terminated in February 1953, during which time approximately 63,500 units were built.

The 8hp Model L was Deere's entry into the "baby tractor" market. Deere Archives

Overview of the Model G

At introduction, the Model G closely resembled the Models A and B tractors. Within one year, however, any possibility of confusion was dismissed as Deere introduced the styled versions of the A and B, but maintained the unstyled look for the Model G.

The Model G was produced in both unstyled and styled versions; low-radiator versions; and equipped with four- and six-speed transmissions. Unlike the A and B Series, the G Series was offered in an all-fuel version only.

While Deere eventually offered the Model G in tricycle, narrow, wide, and high-crop configura-

A Heavy-Duty General Purpose Tractor of Comparatively Light Weight

Simple — Dependable — Long-Lived

The outstanding advantage of the John Deere Model "G" Tractor is its powerful, smooth-running, two-cylinder engine, making possible the utmost simplicity and a minimum of parts to require adjustment and eventual replacement.

Fewer and heavier parts last longer, give the tractor longer life. Maintenance cost is lower, and you can make the majority of required adjustments yourself.

Because of the exclusive design of the two-cylinder engine, the Model "G" burns low-cost fuels successfully, just as have all other John Deere Tractors over a period of many years. This is a material saving. The power of the engine is delivered directly to the drive wheels through spur gears, without bevel gears which consume power. On belt work every ounce of engine power is delivered to the pulley which is mounted right on the crankshaft.

The life of the engine is guarded by a full-pressure force-feed lubricating system with oil-filter, oil wash-down air cleaner, crankcase breather and ventilator, fuel filter and a complete enclosure of all working parts. The Model "G" will give long-time satisfaction.

A Pleasure to Operate

You will find the Model "G" Tractor easy to operate. The two-cylinder, valve-in-head engine has plenty of power, plenty of ability to "hang on" under sustained loads, and it operates with the utmost smoothness. Care in weighing and balancing pistons and connecting rods, care in balancing the rugged crankshaft, flywheel, and belt pulley assembly, statically as well as dynamically, with control exercised by the sensitive governor, assures smooth flowing power. It is really a pleasure to operate the John Deere Model "G" General Purpose Tractor.

Extra-Value Features

There are many extra-value features built into the John Deere Model "G" Tractor. There are heavier parts, stronger parts all the way through. A new, manually controlled radiator shutter, with guard, can be operated from the tractor platform. The operator can easily maintain accurate engine temperature, on cold days or hot, going with the wind or against it, which means more uniform engine performance and an even greater measure of operating economy.

Foot-controlled differential brakes, ample clearance under the axles, 60- to 84-inch adjustment of rear wheel tread, convenient hitch which is fully adjustable vertically and horizontally and which remains permanently on the tractor, built-in power shaft, and the most modern hydraulic power lift . . . these are all features which save labor, cut your farming costs, and speed up your work.

Four-Speed Transmission

To obtain any one of four forward speeds, or reverse, simply operate the single gear shift lever. Speeds, when tractor is equipped with 51½-inch steel wheels, are: (1st) 2¼ m.p.h., (2nd) 3¾ m.p.h., (3rd) 4¾ m.p.h., (4th) 6 m.p.h., and (reverse) 3 m.p.h.

Regular steel wheels, skeleton steel wheels, and wheels with low-pressure tires are all available upon order. There is, of course, a wide variety of lugs, guide bands and extension rims.

More Work at Lower Cost

The Model "G" will especially appeal to the large-acreage corn grower because of its ability to handle a three-bottom plow, large disk harrow, four-row cultivator, two-row mounted corn picker, and to provide ample and steady belt power for threshing, grinding feed, pumping, and similar jobs.

The large-acreage cotton grower will appreciate it because of its ability to handle three-row bedders under all conditions, and four-row bedders under many conditions, four-row planters and cultivators.

The grain grower who also raises some corn or cotton will like it because it will handle row-crop work in addition to all the jobs necessary to the growing of small grains.

See the New John Deere Model "G" General Purpose Tractor at your dealer's store. Arrange for a field demonstration. Increase your yearly profit by cutting operating costs from plowing and planting time right on to the end of the harvest season.

Get the Feel of the Wheel...Ask Your Dealer for a Demonstration

Model G was available with either steel wheels or rubber tires. During World War II, when rubber was in short

supply, many new tractors were delivered with four-speed transmission and steel wheels. Deere and Co.

Trends in US Wheel Tractor Sales 1937–1940

Year	Wheel Tractors Sold (Total)	Row-Crop Tractors Sold (Total)	Row-Crop Tractors As % of Wheel Tractors	Row-Crop Tractors Sold Under 30 Belt hp	As % of GP Tractors	Row-Crop Tractors Sold 30 + Over Belt hp	As % of GP Tractors
1937	216,169	183,656	84.9%	173,659	94.6%	9,997	5.4%
1938	141,593	127,076	89.7%	116,381	91.5%	10,625	8.5%
1939	157,497	147,206	93.4%	140,281	95.2%	6,925	4.8%
1940	215,673	205,489	95.3%	185,006	90.1%	20,843	9.9%

tions, the two-wheel tricycle-front stood alone until 1947. That year, the single-wheel Model GN and the adjustable front tread Model GW joined the line-up. In 1950, the high-crop Model GH was added.

G Series Engine

The decision to build the Model G was made in January 1937. As part of that decision, Deere engineers stated their parameters for the design of the Model G engine: "The engine design follows our successfully established practice of two-cylinder construction with the ability to satisfactorily burn low cost fuels, thermo syphon cooling, and pressure lubrication to all bearings. The engine is 6$\frac{1}{8}$in bore x 7in stroke, valve in head type, operating at 975rpm and delivering an operating maximum of 34 brake horsepower with fuel consumption of less

Early low-radiator Model G debuted with maximum 35.91hp at the belt pulley. Deere Archives

Low-radiator Model G with three-bottom experimental plow; August 1938. Deere Archives

The Model G closely resembles the unstyled Models A and B. It can be easily distinguished, however, in that the frame bulges at the side to accommodate its larger motor. Also, the shift lever quadrant is unique to the Model G. This unit is shown with mounted Cuban cultivator; February 1938. Deere Archives

The Model G provided adequate power to drive the Model 17 combine. Deere Archives

than 0.68 pounds per brake horsepower hour." In almost every way, the engine fitted to the G Series was identical to that fitted to the Models A, B, and D, only built on a larger scale.

The Model G engine was fitted with an Edison-Splitdorf Model CD-2 magneto and a Schebler Model DLTX-24 carburetor with 2¼in throat. Air intake was positioned on the left-hand side of the engine, with the exhaust stack directly opposite. Both stacks passed through the hood.

Unlike the engines of the GP, A, and B models, displacement of the Model G engine was never increased. However, its head was modified to prevent exhaust valve damage early in the tractor's production and, according to *Two-Cylinder*, the block, cylinder head, and upper water pipe were redesigned to facilitate cooling at serial number 7100.

The Model G was tested twice at Nebraska. In its first test of November 15–19, 1937 (Official

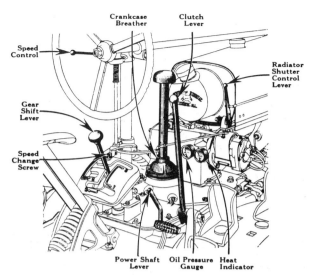

The Model G shift quadrant was unique among the Deere general-purpose line. Deere and Co.

Steel wheels with spade lugs were standard on early Model G. Deere Archives

Drive-wheel option included spoke wheels with tires.
Deere Archives

Tractor Test No. 295), under rated load the engine generated 31.44hp at the belt pulley and 20.70hp at the drawbar. The test tractor was fitted with a four-speed transmission and steel wheels with extension rims and lugs.

The Model G was tested again in 1947. This test tractor was equipped with a six-speed transmission and cast-iron wheels with 12-38 six-ply Firestone tires. In this second test (Official Tractor Test No. 383) of June 5–16, the engine was rated at 33.83 belt hp and 27.01 drawbar hp, an increase of 30 percent at the drawbar.

Success of the Model G

Significantly fewer Model G tractors were sold than Models A or B. However, the tractor should be considered a success in that it pioneered the way for high-horsepower row-crop tractors.

The Model G was the first in a new classification, the over-30hp general-purpose tractor. As shown in the chart, by 1941 this class of tractor had captured nearly 10 percent of the total wheel tractor market.

Transmission

The Model G was originally equipped with a transmission that featured four forward speeds and one reverse speed: first, 2¼mph; second, 3¼mph; third, 4¼mph; fourth 6mph; and reverse, 3mph.

In 1942, a six-speed transmission was introduced that employed a two lever, "Hi" and "Lo"

Cast wheels became the standard in later Model Gs.
Deere Archives

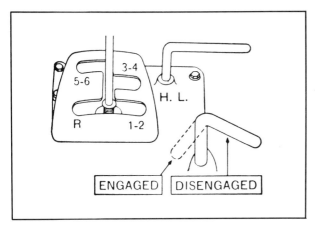

Model G PTO controls.

Belt power at work in Idaville, Indiana; August, 1937. Deere Archives

range and offered these speeds: first, 2½mph; second, 3½mph; third, 4½mph; fourth, 6½mph; fifth, 8¾mph; sixth, 12½mph; and reverse, 3¼mph.

Both versions of the Model G transmission were fitted with a shift lever quadrant.

Wheel and Tire Options

The standard drive wheels originally were 51½x7in steel wheels with spade lugs. Front wheels were 24x5in steel, reversible disks. Optional drive wheels and rubber tires included: steel-spoke wheels with either 10-36 or 11.25-36

six-ply tires, or cast wheels with a choice of 10-38, 10-36, 11-38, 11.25-36, or 12-38 six-ply tires. The optional front tires were 6-16 four-ply.

In 1942, when the tractor was restyled and fitted with the six-speed transmission, rubber tires became standard. Spoke wheels fitted with

Model G featured standard PTO. This model is providing power to a Model 616 hay press. Deere Archives

Model G with three-row bedder. Deere Archives

Model G could disk up to ten acres an hour. Shown with 20ft basin disk harrow. Deere Archives

rubber tires were no longer featured, and steel-spoke wheels with lugs were classified as special equipment.

Wheel and tire options in 1942 included cast drive wheels fitted with either 10-38, 11-38, or 12-38 six-ply tires. Steel-spoke wheels were offered with the four-speed transmission only. Front tires were 6-16 four-ply rubber. Steel-spoke wheels with guide bands were available in a 24x5in size.

Final Drive and Rear Wheel Tread

With the exception of the high-crop version, the G Series was fitted with all-spur-gear transmission with four steps of reduction. Its rear tread was adjustable between 60 and 84in. In addition, optional rear axles were available which enabled a range of tread widths of 60 to 88in and 68 to 112in.

Hydraulic Lift, Belt Pulley, and Power Shaft

Hydraulic power lift was an option on the Model G. Belt pulley and power takeoff were standard features. The company promoted the Model G as having "ample and steady belt power for threshing, grinding feed, pumping and similar jobs."

Model G with four-row planter could plant up to sixty acres a day. Deere Archives

Model G pulling two-row potato planter. Deere Archives

Model G with Model 25-A mounted two-row corn picker;
August 1938. Deere Archives

Drawbar Performance

A genuine three-plow tractor, the Model G was promoted by Deere as having been "Built for the Large Acreage Row-Crop Farmer . . . designed to pull three 14in plows under average conditions. It will develop sufficient belt power to operate machines up to and including a 28in thresher, under ordinary conditions. . . . Here is a powerful general purpose tractor . . . built to the high John Deere standards of ruggedness, adaptability, long life, and economical operation."

Deere advertised the tractor as doing "more work at lower cost." The company exploited this significant feature in an effort to sell the unit as the "primary" tractor for small-grain growers.

Advertisements declared, "The grain grower who also raises some corn or cotton will like it because it will handle row-crop work in addition to all the jobs necessary to the growing of small grains."

Deere further promoted the tractor as having "the daily work output of ten to twelve horses or mules," and being capable of plowing twelve acres; disking twenty-five to thirty-five acres with a 10ft double disk or disking seventy-five to 100 acres with a 21ft single disk; listing or bedding thirty-five to fifty acres; planting sixty acres with a four-row planter; cultivating forty to sixty acres with a four-row cultivator; cutting twenty-five to thirty-five acres with a power mower; harvesting forty to fifty or more acres with a 10ft grain binder; picking ten to eighteen acres with a two-row corn picker; pulling a two-row potato digger; and operating a threshing machine with a 28in threshing cylinder.

Unstyled Model G and two-row potato digger with direct hitch. Deere Archives

Low-Radiator Model G, Model GM, and Other Modifications

Under certain conditions, the early Model G suffered from overheating problems. According to *Two-Cylinder*, overheating was more common in the South than it was in the North.

Soon after the problem surfaced, Deere engineers set about to correct it. A larger-capacity radiator was designed and fitted to tractors at serial number 4251. Approximately 3,000 units were built before the change, and these tractors are referred to as low-radiator units.

The change in radiator required modifications to the radiator shutter, fan, shroud, and hood. In addition, water capacity was increased from 11 to 13 gallons.

The company developed a field-modification package so that tractors in the field could be easily updated. As a result, the low-radiator Model G is extremely rare and thus is highly valued by enthusiasts.

In 1942, the unstyled Model G was replaced by a styled unit, designed by Dreyfuss. At the same time, it was also made available with a six-speed transmission. Because of price controls imposed by the federal government due to World War II, it was necessary that a proposed price increase for the styled unit be approved. The appropriate application was made, but the price increase was denied. Deere sidestepped price regulations by designating the restyled unit the Model GM.

The GM was presented as a new machine, whose price did not have to be evaluated relative to a model previously in production. In 1947, when price controls were lifted, the tractor was redesignated the Model G.

The late Model G was updated at the introduction of the Models GN and GW in 1947, in much the same manner as Deere's other tractors. It was fitted with a cushioned operator seat with back-rest, the battery was relocated beneath the seat, and electric start and lights were offered as stan-

In 1942, the Model G was restyled and designated the Model GM. Deere Archives

A New and Finer
JOHN DEERE
3-PLOW TRACTOR
Model "GM"

*New in its styled lines . . .
six forward speeds . . .
electric starter and
lights . . . ramped
head engine . . . im-
proved operating efficiency . . . ease of
attaching equipment*

Although it was basically identical to the Model G, but featured restyling and optional six-speed transmission, the Model GM was introduced as a new tractor model in 1941. Deere and Co.

Model GH was the high-crop version of the GW.

Late-styled Model G. Cushioned seat, lights, and electric starting were standard. Pictured with a Model 72 forage harvester. Deere Archives

dard equipment. Both Powr-Trol remote hydraulics and a Roll-O-Matic front end were also offered.

Models GN, GW, and GH

In 1947, Deere added single-front-wheel and adjustable front-end versions of the Model G, designated the GN and GW, respectively.

The Model GN was fitted with a single 7.50x16in eight-ply tire. The Model GW was fitted with a front end adjustable between 48 and 80in. Standard front tires were 6.00x16in six-ply.

In 1947, the company made available a two-piece front pedestal and interchangeable front ends for the Model G, as well as for the A and B models. Front-wheel equipment available for the G with the convertible pedestal included a single front wheel; a two-wheel tricycle front available with or without Roll-O-Matic; a 38in fixed-tread axle; and an adjustable axle with tread adjustment between 48 and 80in.

In 1950, Deere introduced the Model GH, a high-crop version of the GW. Greater height was achieved in the front through use of longer front axle knees and spindles. The spindle on the GH was 28$\frac{1}{4}$in, versus 19$\frac{3}{4}$in on the GW.

In order to achieve greater height in the rear, the GH model required a unique driveshaft housing, along with unique rear axles, differential, and final drive housings and components. As final drive reductions could not be achieved through gearing, the transfer of power from the differential to final drive was by means of sprockets and roller chain.

Reportedly, of the fewer than 250 units of the GH built, only six are known to exist today. Indeed, it is one of the rarest John Deere tractors.

Specifications: John Deere Model G Three-Plow General Purpose Tractor

Horsepower	Three 14in plows, or 28in John Deere thresher operating under normal conditions
Speeds	First, 2$\frac{1}{4}$mph; second, 3$\frac{1}{4}$mph; third, 4$\frac{1}{4}$mph; fourth, 6mph; reverse, 3mph
Belt pulley	12$\frac{3}{4}$in diameter, 8$\frac{1}{2}$ face, 975rpm, one roller and one bronze bearing
Belt speed	3,270fpm
Engine	Two cylinders, cast-in-block, valves-in-head
	Speed: 975rpm
	Bore and stroke: 6$\frac{1}{8}$x7in
	Crankshaft: Special-quality steel, drop-forged, 3$\frac{3}{8}$in crank pins
	Main bearings: Two bronze-backed, Babbitt-lined, removable, 3in diameter, 3$\frac{1}{2}$in width
	Connecting rod bearings: Special-quality steel, drop-forged; Babbitt bearings centrifugally spun in rod, 3$\frac{3}{8}$in diameter, 2$\frac{5}{8}$in width; bronze bushings for piston pins
	Governor: John Deere design, enclosed fly-ball type with one ball thrust and two self-adjusting ball bearings
	Carburetor: Natural-draft type with load and idle adjustment
	Ignition: High-tension magneto with enclosed automatic impulse starter
	Air cleaner: Oil-wash type
	Lubrication: Full force-feed pressure system with oil filter
	Cooling: Thermo-syphon with gear- and shaft-driven fan (no belts or water pump)
Fuel tank capacity	Fuel: 17 gallons
	Gasoline: 1$\frac{1}{2}$ gallons
Water capacity	11 gallons
Clutch	Four 10in dry disks, locking in and out
Transmission	Selective type, spur gears, forged, cut, and heat-treated; shafts operating on four ball, four taper, and seven roller bearings
Rear axles	3$\frac{1}{4}$in diameter; mounted on four tapered roller bearings
Rear wheel size	51$\frac{1}{2}$in diameter, 7in face
Front wheel size	24in diameter, 5in face; mounted on four tapered roller bearings
Rear wheel tread	60 to 84in
Wheelbase	90$\frac{1}{4}$in
Turning radius	8ft, 6in
Drawbar adjustment	Vertical adjustment: 10$\frac{3}{16}$ and 15in
	Horizontal adjustment: 24$\frac{3}{4}$in
	Lengthwise adjustment: 9in

Specifications: John Deere Model G Three-Plow General Purpose Tractor

Power takeoff speed 532rpm
Dimensions Overall width: 84in
Overall length: 135in
Height to radiator cap: 61$\frac{1}{2}$in
Shipping weight 4,400lb
Source: Deere Publication Series A370 of 1937.

Specifications: John Deere Model G General Purpose Tractor

Horsepower Three 14in plow bottoms or a four-bottom bedder under normal conditions
Speeds First, 2$\frac{1}{3}$mph; second, 3$\frac{1}{3}$mph; third, 4$\frac{1}{2}$mph; fourth, 6$\frac{1}{3}$mph; reverse,
3$\frac{1}{4}$mph
Belt pulley 12$\frac{3}{4}$in diameter, 8$\frac{1}{2}$in face, 975rpm; one roller and one bronze bearing
Belt speed 3,270fpm
Engine Two cylinders, cast-in-block, valves-in-head
Speed: 975rpm
Bore and stroke: 6$\frac{1}{8}$x7in
Crankshaft: Special-quality steel, drop-forged, 3$\frac{3}{8}$in crank pins
Bearings: Two main, bronze-backed, Babbitt-lined, removable, 3in diameter,
3$\frac{1}{2}$in length
Connecting rods: Special-quality steel, drop-forged; Babbitt bearings,
centrifugally spun in rod, 3$\frac{3}{8}$in diameter, 2$\frac{5}{8}$in width; bronze bushing for
piston pin
Governor: John Deere design, enclosed fly-ball with one ball thrust and two
self-adjusting ball bearings
Carburetor: Natural-draft type with load and idle adjustment
Ignition: High-tension magneto with enclosed automatic impulse starter
Air cleaner: Oil-wash type
Lubrication: Full force-feed pressure system with oil filter
Cooling: Thermo-siphon with gear- and shaft-driven fan (no belts or water
pump)
Fuel tank capacity Fuel: 17 gallons
Gasoline: 1$\frac{1}{2}$ gallons
Water capacity 11 gallons
Clutch Four 10in dry disks, locking in and out
Transmission Selective type, spur gears, forged, cut, and heat-treated; shafts operating on
seven roller, four tapered, four ball bearings
Rear axles 3$\frac{1}{4}$in diameter; mounted on four tapered roller bearings
Rear wheels Tire sizes/wheel equipment:
11-38* six-ply/cast wheels
12-38 six-ply/cast wheels
11-38* six-ply tires, mounted on cast wheels; recommended for average field
conditions; steel-spoke wheels with lugs were available as special equipment;
51$\frac{1}{2}$in diameter, 7in face
Front wheel size 6.00x16in four-ply rubber tires; mounted on four tapered roller bearings; steel-
spoke wheels with guide bands available as special equipment, 24in
diameter; spoke wheels with guide bands available as special equipment,
24in diameter, 5in face
Rear wheel tread 60 to 84in
Wheelbase 90$\frac{1}{4}$in
Drawbar adjustment Vertical adjustment: 10$\frac{1}{4}$ to 15in
Horizontal adjustment: 24$\frac{3}{4}$in
Lengthwise adjustment: 9in
Power takeoff speed 532rpm
Dimensions Overall width: 84$\frac{3}{4}$in
Overall length: 135in

Specifications: John Deere Model G General Purpose Tractor

Overall height: 86³/₄in

Height to radiator cap: 64³/₈in

Shipping weight   4,928lb

Note: Dimensions and weight are based on 11-38 six-ply tires mounted on cast wheels.

Source: Deere Publication Series A456 of 1941.

Specifications: John Deere Model GM Tractor

Horsepower	Three 14in plow bottoms or a four-bottom bedder under normal conditions
Speeds	First, 2¹/₂mph; second, 3¹/₂mph; third, 4¹/₂mph; fourth, 6¹/₃mph; fifth, 8¹/₂mph; sixth, 12mph; reverse, 3¹/₄mph
Belt pulley	12³/₄in diameter, 8¹/₂in face, 975rpm; one roller and one bronze bearing
Belt speed	3,270fpm
Engine	Two cylinders, cast-in-block, valves-in-head
	Speed: 975rpm
	Bore and stroke: 6¹/₈x7in
	Crankshaft: Special-quality steel, drop-forged, 3³/₈in crank pins
	Main bearings: Two main, bronze-backed, Babbitt-lined, removable, 3in diameter, 3¹/₂in width
	Connecting rods: Special-quality steel, drop-forged; Babbitt bearings, centrifugally spun in rod, 3³/₈in diameter, 2⁵/₈in width; bronze bushings for piston pin
	Governor: John Deere design, enclosed fly-ball type with one ball thrust and two self-adjusting ball bearings
	Carburetor: Natural-draft type with load and idle adjustment
	Ignition: High-tension magneto with enclosed automatic impulse starter
	Air cleaner: Oil-wash type
	Lubrication: Full force-feed pressure system with oil filter
	Cooling: Thermo-syphon with gear- and shaft-driven fan (no belts or water pump)
Fuel tank capacity	Fuel: 17 gallons
	Gasoline: 1¹/₂ gallons
Water capacity	13 gallons
Clutch	Four 10in dry disks, locking in and out
Transmission	Selective-type spur gears, forged, cut, and heat-treated; shafts operating on seven roller, four tapered, and four ball bearings
Rear axles	3¹/₄in diameter; mounted on four tapered roller bearings
Rear wheels	Tire sizes/wheel equipment:
	10-38 six-ply mounted on cast wheels
	11-38* six-ply mounted on cast wheels
	12-38 six-ply mounted on cast wheels
	11-38* six-ply mounted on cast wheels; recommended for average field conditions; steel-spoke wheels with lugs available as special equipment, 51¹/₂in diameter, 7in face (furnished with four speeds only)
Front wheel size	6.00x16in four-ply rubber tires mounted on four tapered roller bearings; steel-spoke wheels with guide bands available as special equipment, 24in diameter, 5in face
Rear wheel tread	60 to 84in
Wheelbase	91in
Turning radius	8ft, 6in
Drawbar adjustment	Vertical adjustment: 12¹/₂ to 17³/₈in
	Horizontal adjustment: 24³/₄in
	Lengthwise adjustment: 12¹/₂in
Power takeoff speed	532rpm
Dimensions	Overall width: 84³/₄in

Specifications: John Deere Model GM Tractor

	Overall length: 137⁷⁄₁₆in
	Overall height: 86⁷⁄₈in
	Height to radiator cap: 65⁷⁄₈in
Shipping weight	5,100lb (est.)

Source: Deere Publication Series A456 of 1941.

Specifications: John Deere Model G General Purpose Tractor

Horsepower	All-fuel engine: Maximum 36.01hp on the drawbar
	All-fuel engine: Maximum 39.80hp on the belt
Speeds	First, 2¹⁄₂mph; second, 3¹⁄₂mph; third, 4¹⁄₂mph; fourth, 6¹⁄₂mph; fifth, 8³⁄₄mph; sixth, 12¹⁄₂mph; reverse, 3¹⁄₂mph
Belt pulley	Regular equipment, 12³⁄₄in diameter, 8¹⁄₂in face, 975rpm
Belt speed	3,270fpm
Power takeoff speed	Conforms to ASAE power takeoff standards
Engine	Two cylinders, cast-in-block, valves-in-head
	Speed: 975rpm
	Bore and stroke: 6¹⁄₈x7in
	Main bearings: Two bronze-backed, Babbitt-lined, removable, 3in diameter, 3¹⁄₂in width
	Connecting rod bearings: Babbitt, centrifugally spun in rod, 3³⁄₈in diameter, 2⁵⁄₈in width
	Governor: John Deere design, enclosed fly-ball with one ball thrust and two self-adjusting ball bearings
	Carburetor: Natural-draft type with load and idle adjustment
	Ignition: Battery-distributor, regular; high-tension magneto with enclosed automatic impulse starter, optional
	Air cleaner: Oil-wash type
	Lubrication: Full force-feed pressure system with oil filter
	Cooling: Thermo-siphon with gear-driven fan (no belts or water pump)
Starting and lighting	Regular equipment, twelve-volt system with voltage regulator; two front lights and one rear light
Fuel tank capacity	Fuel: 17 gallons
	Gasoline: 1¹⁄₂ gallons
Water capacity	13 gallons
Clutch	Four 10in dry disks, locking in and out
Rear axles	3¹⁄₄in diameter; mounted on four tapered roller bearings
Rear tires and wheels	12-38 six-ply, on cast wheels
Front tires and wheels	6.00x16 four-ply; disk wheels reversible
Rear wheel tread	60 to 84in*
	Note: Tread applies to standard axle. Two special axles can be furnished to provide rear-wheel tread widths of 60 to 88in and 69 to 104in, respectively.
Wheelbase	91in
Turning radius	8ft, 6in
Drawbar adjustments	Conform to ASAE standards
Dimensions	Overall width: 84³⁄₄in
	Overall length: 137⁷⁄₁₆in
	Overall height: 86⁷⁄₈in
	Height to radiator cap: 65⁷⁄₈in
Shipping weight	5,624lb with power lift and cast rear wheels

Source: Deere publication *John Deere General Purpose Tractors (Models A and B) of 1947.*

Specifications: John Deere Model GN General Purpose Tractor

Horsepower	Three 14in plow bottoms or a four-bottom bedder under normal conditions
	Maximum belt hp: 38.10
	Maximum drawbar hp: 34.49
	Maximum pull (second gear): 3,734lb at 3.22mph
Speeds	Forward: $2\frac{1}{2}$, $3\frac{1}{2}$, $4\frac{1}{2}$, $6\frac{1}{2}$, $8\frac{3}{4}$, and $12\frac{1}{2}$mph on 12-38 six-ply tires; reverse: $3\frac{1}{4}$mph
Engine	Two cylinders, cast-in-block, valves-in-head
	Speed: 975rpm (load)
	Bore and stroke: $6\frac{1}{8}$x7in
	Displacement: 413ci
	Compression ratio: 4.20:1
	Carburetor: Natural-draft type with load and idle adjustment
	Ignition: High-tension magneto or battery distributor
	Spark plugs: 18mm Champion No. 8 Com. C
	Lubrication: Full force-feed pressure system with Purolator oil filter element
	Oil capacity:11 quarts
	Cooling: Thermo-syphon with gear- and shaft-driven fan (no belts or water pump)
	Air cleaner: Oil-wash type
Fuel tank capacity	Gravity-feed fuel system; fuel: 17 gallons; gasoline: $1\frac{1}{2}$ gallons
Water capacity	$12\frac{7}{8}$ gallons
Clutch	Hand-operated, four 10in dry disks, locking in and out
Belt pulley	$12\frac{3}{4}$in diameter, $8\frac{1}{2}$ width, 975rpm
Belt speed	3,270fpm
Transmission	Speeds: Six forward and one reverse
	Gears: Selective-type, straight spur, forged, cut, and heat-treated
	Bearings: Shafts operate on seven Hyatt rollers, four Timken tapered, and four New Departure ball bearings
	Oil capacity: 7 gallons
Rear axles	$3\frac{1}{4}$in diameter; mounted on four Timken tapered roller bearings
Rear wheels	12-38 six-ply tires, mounted on cast wheels; recommended for average field conditions
Rear wheel brakes	Two automotive-type internal expanding rear wheel brakes
Power takeoff speed	Shaft diameter $1\frac{3}{4}$in; 532rpm; splined end $19\frac{3}{4}$in above ground, $1\frac{9}{16}$in to right of centerline of tractor, and 14in ahead of hitch; conforms with ASAE standards
Front wheels	7.50x16in eight-ply tire; wheel mounted on two Timken tapered roller bearings
Dimensions	Overall height: $89\frac{1}{2}$in
	Height to radiator cap: $67\frac{1}{8}$in
	Overall length: $140\frac{13}{16}$in
	Width over axles:84in
	Tread adjustment: 60 to 84in
	Clearance: $26\frac{1}{2}$in
Wheelbase	$91\frac{1}{4}$in
Turning radius	10ft, 4in
Shipping weight	5,694lb

Source: Deere publication OM-R2009.

Specifications: John Deere Model GW General Purpose Tractor

Horsepower	Three 14in plow bottoms or a four-bottom bedder under normal conditions
	Maximum belt hp: 38.10
	Maximum drawbar hp: 34.49
	Maximum pull (second gear): 3,734lb at 3.22mph
Speeds	Forward: $2\frac{1}{2}$, $3\frac{1}{2}$, $4\frac{1}{2}$, $6\frac{1}{2}$, $8\frac{3}{4}$, and $12\frac{1}{2}$mph on 12-38 six-ply tires; reverse: $3\frac{1}{4}$mph
Engine	Two cylinders, cast-in-block, valves-in-head
	Speed: 975rpm (load)
	Bore and stroke: $6\frac{1}{8}$x7in
	Displacement: 413ci
	Compression ratio: 4.20 to 1
	Carburetor: Natural-draft type with load and idle adjustment
	Ignition: High-tension magneto or battery distributor
	Spark plugs: 18mm Champion No. 8 Com. C
	Lubrication: Full force-feed pressure system with Purolator oil filter element
	Oil capacity: 11 quarts
	Cooling: Thermo-syphon with gear- and shaft-driven fan (no belts or water pump)
	Air cleaner: Oil-wash type
Fuel tank capacity	Gravity-feed fuel system; fuel: 17 gallons; gasoline: $1\frac{1}{2}$ gallons
Water capacity	$12\frac{7}{8}$ gallons
Clutch	Hand-operated, four 10in dry disks, locking in and out
Belt pulley	$12\frac{3}{4}$in diameter, $8\frac{1}{2}$ width, 975rpm
Belt speed	3,270fpm
Transmission	Speeds: Six forward and one reverse
	Gears: Selective-type, straight spur gears, forged, cut, and heat-treated
	Bearings: Shafts operate on seven Hyatt Rollers, four Timken tapered, and four New Departure ball bearings
	Oil capacity: 7 gallons
Rear axles	$3\frac{1}{4}$in diameter; mounted on four Timken tapered roller bearings
Rear wheels	12-38 six-ply tires, mounted on cast wheels; recommended for average field conditions
Rear wheel brakes	Two automotive-type internal expanding rear wheel brakes
Power takeoff	Shaft diameter $1\frac{3}{4}$in; 532rpm; splined end $19\frac{3}{4}$in above ground, $1\frac{9}{16}$in to right of centerline of tractor, and 14in ahead of hitch; conforms with ASAE standards
Front wheels	6.00x16in six-ply tires; wheels mounted on four Timken tapered roller bearings
Dimensions	Overall height: $88\frac{1}{8}$in
	Height to radiator cap: $68\frac{1}{2}$in
	Overall length: $145\frac{11}{16}$in
	Width over axles:84in
	Tread adjustment: 60 to 84in
	Clearance: $26\frac{1}{2}$in
Wheelbase	$97\frac{3}{8}$in
Turning radius	16ft, 8in
Shipping weight	5,974lb

Source: Deere publication OM-R2009.

Chapter 8

John Deere Model H

In 1935, 40 percent of American farms were smaller than fifty acres—a huge market of 2,694,426 farms. Yet, this market was largely ignored by tractor manufacturers, which built tractors better suited to larger farms.

Consequently, when it came to meeting their horsepower needs, smaller row-crop farmers had three choices: purchase a new tractor that was too large and therefore inefficient; purchase a used tractor; or continue to operate with a horse or mule.

In most cases a new tractor was out of the question, and a used tractor, if too large, remained inefficient. As a result, the small farmer continued to farm with horses or mules.

The $500 Tractor

In the pages of *Farm Implement News,* the call went out for an inexpensive row-crop tractor that would sell for under $500. In 1935, a new Deere Model B tractor fitted with steel wheels listed for $650.

In December 1937, the call was answered when Allis-Chalmers introduced its Model B. Print ads bore the headline "On Rubber, $495 F.O.B. factory," and the B became an instant success.

A high-clearance, four-wheel, true row-crop tractor, it offered 23in minimum clearance under its arched front axle. It straddled a single row, with adjustable rear wheels to 40, 44, 48, and 52in centers.

The engine had four cylinders with bore and stroke of 3¼x3½in with valves in head. Its three-speed transmission offered gear speeds of 2½, 4, and 8mph. The engine developed 15.68 belt hp on gasoline, and was available both in gas and all-fuel versions. At the drawbar, the engine generated 12.97hp with maximum drawbar pull of 1,473lb. A belt pulley and optional PTO were offered as well.

The potential impact of the Allis-Chalmers Model B was summed up eloquently in the December 30, 1937, issue of *Farm Implement News*: "It is hard to avoid a feeling of understatement when trying to estimate the effect on agriculture of a tractor that will 'do everything' on a small farm and cost not much more than a team and far less to operate. A man might run this Model B 700 hours a year and not pay out more than $40 for distillate and oil. . . .

"Farm power of this sort may be the closing link in the chain making practical rural manufac-

John Deere Selected List Prices

Model	1928	1932	1935	1936	1938	1939	1940	1944	1947	1951	1953
C	$850										
GP		825	925								
GPWT		830									
A			945			1,050			1,653	2,297	
AN				945		1,065			1,735	2,370	
AW				1,000		1,130			1,848	2,504	
B			650			787			1,406	1,870	
BN				675		797			1,471	1,920	
BW				748		867			1,593	2,069	
G					1,125	1,085			1,879		2,132
GN									1,909		2,430
GW									1,970		2,950
GH											3,180
H						595	595	639			
HN							600	641			

turing couple with subsistence farming. The decentralization of industry may receive in the Model B and similar models an impetus whose ultimate end no one can foretell. Power and equipment at the Model B level may place the small farmer on an efficiency parity with the larger producer. . . .

"The 'forgotten farmer'—the little fellow—has been remembered. He can now ride on air, just like his rich neighbor across the road, master of time and season. . . ."

The entire industry took notice of the Allis-Chalmers Model B—Deere and Company included. Within ten months, Deere's Model H was in production, Waterloo's offering to the "forgotten farmer."

Introduction of the Model H

The Model H was introduced with the statement, "Now—for the first time in the history of agriculture—a smaller, lower-priced general purpose tractor of the tricycle type is available to handle every power job on the small farm and many jobs on the large farm at rock-bottom cost," and the declaration, "If you've been using animal power because your jobs or the size of your farm did not justify the purchase of a larger tractor, the new Model 'H' is the tractor you've been waiting for. . . ."

The Model H was a genuine, one-bottom general-purpose tractor built to John Deere's exacting standards, and which handled many jobs on the small farm and large farm alike.

Introduced in 1939, production of the Model H began in October 1938 and was suspended in February 1947, during which time Deere sold approximately 60,000 units.

The Model H was priced initially at $595 FOB Waterloo. By way of comparison, in 1939 the Model G was priced at $1,185, the Model A at $1,050, and the Model B at $786.50.

Experimental Model OX

Prototypes of the Model H were built as early as April 1938, and were designated the OX. As many as twelve machines were built in two groups and in two separate styles.

The first group most likely resembled Deere's unstyled tractors, Models A and B. The second set most likely resembled the eventual production tractor, which bore all the markings of Henry Dreyfuss' styled design.

Overview of the Model H

The Model H was produced in a styled version only: with a three-speed transmission, and with a

Studio artwork depicts pulley-side of Model H. Cast front wheels were replaced by stamped-steel wheels in 1944. Deere Archives

distillate-burning engine only. Four distinct configurations were built:

• The two-wheel, tricycle-front Model H
• The single-tire, narrow-front Model HN
• The wide-front or adjustable-front-axle, high-crop Model HWH
• The single-tire, narrow-front, high-crop Model HNH. Of these models, only the Model H was produced for the entire production run.

H Series Engine

Deere engineers stayed with the horizontal, two-cylinder concept when designing the H Series engine. The desirable mechanical features of the engine were described by the company: "The engine follows our established practice of two-cylinder construction, for operation on tractor fuel, with thermo syphon cooling, and pressure lubrication to all crankshaft bearings. Solid [B]abbitt-lined precision-bored bushings are used in the minimum bearing positions, and steel backed precision bearing shells of the nonadjustable type are used in connecting rods for minimum cost. To promote maximum bearing life, a cast alloy crankshaft is used. The engine is of 3⁹/₁₆in bore and 5in stroke, valve-in-head type, operating at a rated speed of 1400rpm and delivering an operating maximum of 13.5hp with fuel consumption less than 0.620lb per horsepower hour."

While the engine displacement was never altered, changes were made to the motor during the course of production. The change from a cast-alloy crankshaft to a steel drop-forged crankshaft was most significant among them.

Records indicate that the first 104 tractors were built with the cast-alloy crankshaft. These units were either scrapped or modified, presumably due to problems with the crankshaft, as the

Flywheel side of Model H. Note single stack for exhaust and screened vent at side of hood for air intake. Deere Archives

View from the operator's seat. Clutch lever is to the right of steering wheel. Deere Archives

engines of all units built after serial number H1104 featured the forged crankshaft.

Engine spark was generated by an Edison-Splitdorf Model RM-2 magneto. The carburetor was a Marvel-Schebler Model DLTX-26 with 1in throat.

The tractor was fitted with an exhaust stack that passed through the center of the hood. Air intake was through a vent in the forward, left-hand section of the hood. A single-stack arrangement made the Model H unique among its family members.

H Series Engine Rating

The Model H was tested at the University of Nebraska between October 31 and November 10, 1938 (Official Tractor Test No. 312). Equipped with 7.50x32in four-ply tires and 284lb cast-iron weights per rear wheel, the test tractor was rated at 12.97hp on the belt pulley and 9.68hp on the drawbar. Maximum drawbar load was 1,839lb at 11.67hp.

Transmission, Foot Throttle, and Final Drive

The Model H was an ideal tractor for a variety of field work. It was equipped with a three-speed transmission that offered forward speeds of 2½, 3½, and 5¾mph. It was also fitted with a foot throttle that overrode the governor and permitted the tractor to be driven at a road speed of 7½mph.

The Model H driveline featured a two-pinion differential mounted directly to the rear axle

Overhead view of Model H fitted with integral cultivator. Deere Archives

Model H with rear wheels set at 44in for plowing. With wheels reversed and hub clamp on the inside, tread was adjustable to 84in; June 1939. Deere Archives

shafts. This arrangement eliminated the need for multiple gear reductions, which simplified the differential and reduced the cost of the tractor.

Tricycle Front and Adjustable Rear Wheel Tread

The front end of the H model was a two-wheel, tricycle-type fitted with 4.00x15in tires. Prior to serial number 47795, the front wheels were cast iron with five oval-shaped holes at the outer rim. In 1944, Deere switched to the more common stamped-steel wheel.

The rear tread of the Model H was adjustable between 44 and 84in from center to center, with the possibility of any setting in between. When the wheels were placed on the rear axles with the hub clamps on the outside, the wheels were adjustable from 44 to 64in. When they were reversed with the hub clamp on the inside, the wheels were adjustable from 64 to 84in. The narrow setting was ideal for plowing and for vegetables grown in narrow rows. The widest setting was ideal for corn cultivation.

Belt Pulley, Hydraulic Power Lift, PTO, and Special Equipment

A belt pulley was standard equipment on the Model H. It was rated at 700rpm and had a belt speed of 2,245fpm. An optional overpulley for the Model H increased the belt speed to one sufficient to operate such equipment as a No. 10A hammer mill.

Other optional equipment included a PTO; hydraulic power lift; electric starting and lighting, either together or separately; manual radiator shutter control; and fenders.

Model H belt power drove sheller. Deere Archives

Drawbar Performance

The H was advertised as a tractor that would "completely replace animal power," for any size farm: "a tractor with the daily work output of four to six horses or mules—a tractor that [would] handle many . . . horse-drawn tools besides a complete line of specially designed drawn, integral, belt-driven and power take-off machines."

The wide variety of integral equipment especially suited to the Model H included one-bottom plows and bedders; two-row cotton and corn planters; two-row listers; variable-row vegetable planters; two-row cultivators; variable-row beet and bean cultivators; and two-row bean harvesters.

The Model H appealed to many farmers who found it well matched to their horse-drawn equipment. Deere Archives

The H easily handled a variety of equipment, including the PTO-powered corn binder. Deere Archives

Integral equipment matched to the Model H included a one-bottom plow. Deere Archives

The Model H's tapered hood permitted operator an excellent view of cultivator and crop rows. Deere Archives

Lister mounted to Model H; June 1940. Deere Archives

*Model H at work cultivating cabbage near Frankesville,
Wisconsin, 1939.* Deere Archives

The tractor was rated to pull a 16in, one-
bottom plow under normal conditions; a 12in, two-
bottom plow under favorable conditions; in a ten-
hour day plow seven acres; with a single-disk,
twenty-five to thirty acres; with a double-disk,
seventeen to twenty acres; plant twenty to thirty
acres; cultivate twenty to thirty-five acres; mow
twenty-five to thirty-five acres; or cut twenty to
twenty-five acres of grain.

The tractor was easily steered and with differential brakes could make short turns in less than a
7½ft radius. This enabled the operator to work in
tight corners and close to trees or fenceposts.

Model HN Narrow-Front

The HN, a single-wheel, narrow-front version
of the Model H, was introduced in 1940 and
remained in production until 1947.

The HN varied little from the tricycle-front H,
other than its pedestal assembly and yoke which
supported a single 6.00x12in front tire. Its rear
tread was adjustable from 44 to 84in.

In small-acreage, narrow-row operations such
as flower and vegetable farms and truck gardens,
the Model HN was ideal. Its single front wheel
passed easily between the 12 to 16in rows commonly used.

Model H with four-row Model 490 planter; May 1939.
Deere Archives

The H was rated to pull one 16in bottom or, as in this photo, two 12in bottoms. Deere Archives

Production of the HN was limited to about 1,100 units, most of which were shipped to California.

Models HWH and HNH High-Crop, Wide, and Narrow Configurations

Introduced in 1941 and built for less than one year, the HWH and HNH were low-volume, high-clearance tractors built almost exclusively for the California market where vegetables, fruits, and flowers were grown in narrow rows or beds.

The adjustable-front HWH offered two choices of front axle, the standard short and the optional long axle. The latter could be fitted at the factory or furnished separately.

The short axle allowed an adjustable tread from 40 to 52in, in 4in increments. The long axle allowed adjustment between 56 and 68in, also in 4in increments. Clearance under the center of the front axle was 21³/₈in. The front tires fitted to the HWH were the standard 4.00x15in four-ply. To increase clearance at the rear end, the tractor was fitted with 8-38 tires, in place of the standard 7-32s. Clearance at the rear, with drawbar removed, was 16¹/₄in.

The Model HNH was simply a standard HN equipped with the standard 38in wheels fitted to the Model B. To accommodate its nine-hole bolt pattern, the HNH was fitted with a nine-bolt hub in place of the standard seven-bolt hub. The front end of the HNH was not modified from that of the HN, however. For this reason, the tractor's front end is posed downward.

Only 125 units of the Model HWH were built and fewer than forty units of the Model HNH were built. Naturally, both are considered rare among collectors.

Full Line of General-Purpose Tractors

With the introduction of the Model H, Deere offered a full range of general-purpose tractors, ideal for row-crop farmers of any size and for small-grain farmers who diversified their operations by also raising row-crops.

Each of these models offered the same basic design and each delivered power through four avenues: at the drawbar, at the belt pulley, at the PTO, and by way of the hydraulic power lift.

Efficient and economical, they provided dependable, long-term service to their owners—oftentimes to more than one generation of owners.

The Models GP, A, B, G, and H were part of the evolution in farm power that began with steam and is not yet complete. Whatever direction the future of farm power takes, these tractors will long be remembered for their unrivaled contribution to the successful development of twentieth century American agriculture.

The Model H was an ideal second tractor on larger farms, where it efficiently performed jobs such as raking hay. Deere Archives

JOHN DEERE SCORES ANOTHER SMASH HIT

MODEL "HWH" for Bedded Crops

THOUSANDS of farmers have been waiting for this tractor. Built for Western growers, it has the special features you've been looking for, plus the outstanding performance and economy heretofore found only in the John Deere Models "H" and "HN" Tractors.

See the new Model "HWH" at your John Deere dealer's and ask for a demonstration. Turn the page and check the specifications of this new tractor.

OUTSTANDING FEATURES

1. Adjustable front wheel tread.
2. Adjustable rear wheel tread.
3. High clearance for bed work.
4. Unmatched economy, dependability, and ease of operation.
5. Electric starting and lighting equipment available.
6. Hydraulic power lift available.
7. Complete line of integral equipment available.

The Model HWH was built for only one year. Approximately 125 units were built before production was suspended. The tractor was likely a victim of World War II rationing of manufacturing materials. Deere Archives

Specifications: John Deere General Purpose Two-Row Cultivating Tractor

Horsepower
Pulls one 16in plow or one 14in bedder under normal conditions, and a two-bottom 12in plow or a two-bottom 12in bedder under favorable conditions; handles a two-row cultivator

Speeds
First, 2½mph; second, 3½mph; third, 5¾mph; reverse, 1¾mph (road speeds up to 7½mph at 1800rpm)

Belt pulley
12¼in diameter, 4½in face, 700rpm
Note: Belt pulley was standard equipment.

Belt speed
3,270fpm

Engine
Two cylinders, cast-in-block, valves-in-head
Speed: 1400rpm
Bore and stroke: 3⁹/₁₆x5in
Crankshaft: Special-quality alloy steel, 2¹/₆in crank pins
Main bearings: Two steel-backed, precision-type; right-hand 2¹/₁₆in diameter, 2in length; left-hand 2¹/₁₆in diameter, 2¼in length
Connecting rods: Special-quality steel, drop-forged; steel-backed bearings, precision-type, 2¹/₁₆in diameter, 1¹⁷/₃₂in length
Governor: John Deere design, enclosed fly-ball type with one ball thrust and two self-adjusting ball bearings
Carburetor: Natural-draft type with load and idle adjustment
Ignition: High-tension magneto with enclosed automatic impulse starter
Air cleaner: Oil-wash type
Lubrication: Full pressure to main crank pin bearings; oil filter
Cooling: Thermo-siphon with gear- and shaft-driven fan (no belts or water pump)

Fuel tank capacity
Fuel: 7½ gallons
Gasoline: ⁷/₈ gallon

Water capacity
5½ gallons

Clutch
Two 9¼in dry disks, locking in and out

Transmission
Selective-type, spur gears, forged, cut and heat-treated; shafts operating on two tapered roller and two roller bearings

Rear axles
2¹/₈in diameter; mounted on four tapered roller bearings

Rear wheel size
6.50x32in; pneumatic, with 7.50x32in tires available

Front wheel size
4.00x15in; pneumatic, mounted on two tapered roller bearings

Rear wheel tread
44 to 80in

Wheelbase
76in

Turning radius
7ft, 5in

Drawbar adjustment
Vertical adjustment: 10 and 15in
Horizontal adjustment: 16¾in

Power takeoff speed
546rpm
Note: Power takeoff was extra.

Dimensions
Overall width: 75in
Overall length: 111¼in
Height to radiator cap: 52in

Shipping weight
2,100lb

Source: Deere Publication Series A468 of 1939.

Specifications: John Deere Model H Tractor

Horsepower	One 16in plow bottom or a 14in bedder under normal conditions, and two 12in plow bottoms or a two-bottom bedder under favorable conditions
	Maximum belt hp: 14.84
	Maximum drawbar hp: 12.48
	Maximum pull: 1,839lb at 2.38mph
Speeds	Forward, $2\frac{1}{2}$, $3\frac{1}{2}$, and $5\frac{3}{4}$mph on 9-32 (regular) pneumatic tires; road speed $7\frac{1}{2}$mph at 1800rpm by using foot control; reverse, $1\frac{3}{4}$mph
Engine	Two cylinders, cast-in-block, valves-in-head
	Speed: 1400rpm (load)
	Bore and stroke: $3\frac{9}{16}$x5in
	Displacement: 99.7ci
	Compression ratio: 4.75:1
	Carburetor: Natural-draft type with load and idle adjustment
	Ignition: High-tension magneto with automatic impulse starter
	Spark plugs: 18mm Champion No. 8 Com. C. or Edison Z-19; spark plug gap 0.030in
	Lubrication: Full force-feed pressure system with Purolator oil filter element
	Oil capacity: $4\frac{1}{2}$ quarts
	Cooling: Thermo-syphon with gear- and shaft-driven fan (no belts or water pump)
	Air cleaner: Oil-wash type
Water capacity	$5\frac{1}{2}$ gallons
Fuel tank capacity	Gravity-feed fuel system; fuel: $7\frac{1}{2}$ gallons, gasoline: $\frac{7}{8}$ gallon
Clutch	Hand-operated, two $9\frac{1}{4}$in dry disks, locking in and out
Belt pulley	$12\frac{1}{4}$in diameter, $4\frac{3}{4}$in width, 700rpm
Belt speed	2,245fpm
Transmission	Speeds: Three forward and one reverse; added road speed up to $7\frac{1}{2}$mph
	Gears: Selective-type, straight spur-cut gears, forged, cut, and heat-treated
	Bearings: Shafts operate on two Timken tapered, two Hyatt rollers, and two bronze bearings
	Oil capacity: 3 gallons
Rear axles	$2\frac{1}{8}$in diameter; mounted on four Timken tapered roller bearings
Rear wheels	9-32 four-ply tires; mounted pressed-steel wheels; recommended for average field conditions
Rear wheel brakes	Two automotive-type internal expanding rear wheel brakes
Front wheels	Reversible for added clearance; 4.00x15in four-ply rubber tires mounted on four Timken tapered roller bearings; pressed-steel wheel
Dimensions	On regular 9-32 pneumatic tires:
	Overall height: 73in
	Height to radiator cap: $52\frac{1}{2}$in
	Overall length: $112\frac{1}{2}$in
	Overall width: $79\frac{1}{4}$in;
	Clearance: $20\frac{3}{4}$in
Rear wheel tread	Adjustable from 44 to 84in
Wheelbase	76in
Turning radius	7ft, 5in
Drawbar adjustment	Conforms to ASAE standards
Power takeoff speed	Shaft diameter $1\frac{3}{8}$in; 546rpm; splined end is $25\frac{1}{4}$in above ground, $2\frac{7}{8}$in to left of centerline of tractor and 14in ahead of hitch; conforms to ASAE standards
Shipping weight	2,141lb on 9-32 four-ply pneumatic tires, pressed-steel wheels rear; 4.00x15in four-ply tires front

Source: Deere publication OM-R2011.

Specifications: John Deere Model HN Tractor

Horsepower	One 16in plow bottom or a 14in bedder under normal conditions, and two 12in plow bottoms, or a two-bottom bedder under favorable conditions
Speeds	First, 2$\frac{1}{2}$mph; second, 3$\frac{1}{2}$mph; third, 5$\frac{3}{4}$mph; fourth (road speeds up to 7$\frac{1}{2}$mph at 1800rpm); reverse, 1$\frac{3}{4}$mph
Belt pulley	12$\frac{1}{4}$in diameter, 4$\frac{3}{4}$in face, 700rpm; one roller and one bronze bearing
Belt speed	2,245fpm
Engine	Two cylinders, cast-in-block, valves-in-head
	Speed: 1400rpm
	Bore and stroke: 3$\frac{9}{16}$x5in
	Crankshaft: Special-quality steel, drop-forged, 2$\frac{1}{16}$in crank pin
	Main bearings: Two steel-backed, precision-type; right-hand, 2$\frac{1}{16}$in diameter, 2in length; left-hand, 2$\frac{1}{16}$in diameter, 2$\frac{1}{2}$in length
	Connecting rods: Special-quality steel, drop-forged; Babbitt bearings, centrifugally spun in rod, 2$\frac{1}{16}$in diameter, 1$\frac{17}{32}$in width; bronze bushing on piston pin
	Governor: John Deere design, enclosed fly-ball type with one ball thrust and two self-adjusting ball bearings
	Carburetor: Natural-draft type with load and idle adjustment
	Ignition: High-tension magneto with enclosed automatic impulse starter
	Spark plugs: 18mm Champion No. 8 Com. C. or Edison Z-19; spark plug gap 0.030in
	Air cleaner: Oil-wash type
	Lubrication: Full-pressure system to main and crank-pin bearings; with oil filter
	Cooling: Thermo-syphon with gear- and shaft-driven fan (no belts or water pump)
Fuel tank capacity	Fuel: 7$\frac{1}{2}$ gallons
	Gasoline: $\frac{7}{8}$ gallon
Water capacity	5$\frac{1}{2}$ gallons
Clutch	Two 9$\frac{1}{4}$in dry disks, locking in and out
Transmission	Selective-type spur gears, forged, cut, and heat-treated; shafts operating on two roller, two tapered roller, and two bronze bearings
Rear axles	2$\frac{1}{8}$in diameter; mounted on four Timken tapered roller bearings
Rear wheels	Rubber tires: 9-32 four-ply tires, mounted pressed-steel; other sizes available as special equipment
Front wheel size	6.00x12in six-ply rubber tires mounted on two tapered roller bearings
Rear wheel tread	44 to 84in
Wheelbase	76in
Turning radius	7ft, 5in
Drawbar adjustment	Vertical adjustment: 10 and 15in
	Horizontal adjustment: 16$\frac{3}{4}$in
	Lengthwise adjustment: 4in
Power takeoff speed	546rpm; available as special equipment
Dimensions	Overall width: 79$\frac{1}{4}$in
	Overall length: 112$\frac{1}{2}$in
	Overall height: 73in
	Height to radiator cap: 52$\frac{1}{2}$in
Shipping weight	2,131lb

Note: Dimensions and weight are based on 9-32 four-ply tires mounted on steel wheels.
Source: Deere sales literature of 1945.

Bibliography

Books

Appleyard, John, *The Farm Tractor*, North Pomfret, VT: David and Charles, Incorporated, 1987.

Broehl, Wayne G. Jr., *John Deere's Company: A History of Deere & Company and Its Times*, New York: Doubleday and Company, Incorporated, 1984.

Gray, R. B., *The Agricultural Tractor: 1855–1950*, St. Joseph, MI: American Society of Agricultural Engineers, 1954.

Holbrook, Stewart, *Machines of Plenty*, New York: Macmillan Publishing Company, Incorporated, 1955.

Huber, Donald, *How Johnny Popper Replaced the Horse*, Moline, IL: Deere and Company, 1988.

Jennings, Dana Close, *Farm Steam Shows, USA & Canada*, Aberdeen, SD: North Plains Press, 1972.

Jones, Fred R., *Farm and Gas Engines and Tractors*, New York: McGraw-Hill Book Company, Incorporated, 1938.

Leffingwell, Randy, *The American Farm Tractor*, Osceola, WI: Motorbooks International, Incorporated, 1991.

Macmillan, Don and Russell Jones, *John Deere Tractors and Equipment 1837–1959*, St. Joseph, MI: American Society of Agricultural Engineers, 1988.

Marsh, Barbara, *Corporate Tragedy: The Agony of International Harvester Company*, Doubleday and Company, Incorporated, 1985.

Pierce, Fulkerson, *Farm Tractors of North America 1892–1979*, Sonora, KY: Tractor Comparisons, 1979.

Rasmussen, Henry, *John Deere Tractors: Big Green Machines in Review*, Osceola, WI: Motorbooks International, Incorporated, 1987.

Smith, Harris P., *Farm Machinery and Equipment*, 2nd Edition, New York: McGraw-Hill Book Company, Incorporated, 1937.

Stephens, Randy, *Farm Tractors: 1926–1956*, Overland Park, KS: Intertec Publishing, 1990.

Stephenson, James H., *Traction Farming and Traction Engineering*, Chicago: Frederick J. Drake and Company, 1915.

Vizoil Refining Company, *Farm Tractors: The history of their development with notes on their proper maintenance*, London: TEE Publishing, 1976.

Wendel, C. H., *Encyclopedia of American Farm Tractors*, Sarasota, FL: Crestline Publishing, 1979.

Wik, Reynold M., *Steam Power on the American Farm*, Philadelphia: University of Pennsylvania Press, 1953.

Williams, Michael, *Classic Farm Tractors*, Poole, UK: Blandford Books, Limited, 1984.

Williams, Michael, *Farm Tractors in Colour*, New York: Macmillan Publishing Company, Incorporated, 1974.

Williams, Michael, *Great Tractors*, Poole, UK: Blandford Books, Limited, 1982.

Williams, Robert C., *Fordson, Farmall, and Poppin' Johnny: A History of the Farm Tractor and Its Impact on America*, Urbana, IL: University of Illinois Press, 1987.

Wright, Philip A., *Old Farm Tractors*, North Pomfret, VT: David and Charles, Incorporated, 1962.

Periodicals

"Air-Tired Tractor in Transportation Test," *Farm Implement News*, December 8, 1932: pp18, 23.

Anderson, K. W., "Hydraulic Controls for Farm Implements," *Agricultural Engineering*, August 1946: pp355-356.

"Another Angle on the Tractor Count," *Farm Implement News*, March 3, 1932: pp15.

"Baby Tractors Sell," *Business Week*, July 20, 1940: pp47-48.

Baker, E. J., "A Quarter Century of Tractor Development," *Agricultural Engineering*, June 1931: pp206-207.

Benjamin, B. R., "Farm Requirements of the Small All-Purpose Tractor," *Agricultural Engineering*, May 1937: pp209-212.

"Bought Tractors–Kept Boys," *Farm Implement News*, December 11, 1930: pp17.

"Concerning General Purpose Tractors," *Farm Implement News*, January 16, 1930: pp19.

Coultas, W. J., "The A.S.A.E. Tractor Power Take-off and Drawbar Hitch Standardization Program," *Agricultural Engineering*, August 1944: pp284, 289.

Davidson, J. B., "Possibilities in Tractor Research," *Agricultural Engineering*, December 1927: pp335-336.

"Deere & Co.," *Fortune*, August 1936: pp72-77.

"Discrediting Tractor Knockers," *Farm Implement News*, March 31, 1932: pp8.

"Expenditures for Farm Production," *Farm Implement News*, August 29, 1935: pp20.

"Farm Equipment Companies Are Bigger and Fewer," *Business Week*, May 6, 1931: pp22.

"Farm Implement Rivals Are R'arin'," *Business Week*, March 6, 1937: pp20, 22.

"Farm Tools Boom," *Business Week*, June 6, 1936: pp32-33.

"Farmers' Cash Income for 1936 Estimated at $7,850,000,000," *Farm Implement News*, October 8, 1936: pp34.

"Farms Go Mechanical," *Business Week*, July 1, 1939: pp34-35.

Hawthorn, Fred W., "Farm Tests of Low-Pressure Tractor Tires," *Agricultural Engineering*, February 1934: pp61, 63.

Heitsu, D. C., "Requirements of the Small All-Purpose Tractor from the Implement Engineer's Viewpoint," *Agricultural Engineering*, May 1937: pp213-214.

Heitsu, D. C., "The Requirements of the General-Purpose Tractor," *Agricultural Engineering*, May 1929: pp145-159.

"High Returns in Farming Found with Adequate Farm Equipment," *Farm Implement News*, March 3, 1932: pp14.

"Horses and Mules on Farms," *Farm Implement News*, March 3, 1932: pp15.

"Horses Lacking," *Farm Implement News*, March 28, 1935: pp12.

"Huber General Purpose Tractor," *Farm Implement News*, January 8, 1931: pp29.

"Implements: Machines Make Light Work for Modern Farmer," *Newsweek*, February 6, 1937: pp28, 30.

Iverson, Geo. W., "Possibilities of the All Purpose Tractor," *Agricultural Engineering*, September 1922: pp147-149.

Jasny, Naum, "Tractor versus Horse as a Source of Farm Power," *American Economic Review*, December 1935: pp708-723.

Jones, G. D., "General-Purpose Tractor Design," *Agricultural Engineering*, March 1931: pp91-92.

Josephson, H. B., "Tests of Tractor Wheel Equipment," *Agricultural Engineering*, October 1928: pp313-314.

Kranick, Frank N. G., "Direct Engine-Driven Power Take-Off," *Agricultural Engineering*, June 1948: pp245-248.

Lavers, A. W., "Requirement for the General-Purpose Agricultural Tractor," *Agricultural Engineering*, October 1933: pp279.

Lucas, D. B., "Ease and Comfort in Tractor Operation," *Agricultural Engineering*, October 1929: pp313.

McCuen, G. W., "Latest Developments in the Motorization of Corn Production," *Agricultural Engineering*, October 1927: pp279-281.

Mowitz, Dave, "Ageless Iron: Restoring Your Legacy," *Successful Farming*, mid-February 1991: pp27-31, 34-37, 40-42.

Murphy, Roy E., "Operating an Iowa Farm without Horses," *Agricultural Engineering*, March 1925: pp59-60.

Olney, Raymond, "Standardization of Farm Equipment," *Agricultural Engineering*, January 1920: pp4-5, 18.

"Percentage of Rubber-Tired Tractors," *Farm Implement News*, November 19, 1936: pp15.

"Points in Favor of Air Tires on Tractors," *Farm Implement News*, June 21, 1934: pp23.

"Power Farming Tendencies in 1929," *Farm Implement News*, January 9, 1930: pp18-20.

"Records Prove Lower Tractor Operating Costs on Corn Farms," *Farm Implement News*, August 13, 1931: pp20-22.

"Sears to Push Tractors," *Farm Implement News*, January 7, 1932: pp15.

Shawl, R. I., "Mechanical Equipment in Corn Cultivation," *Agricultural Engineering*, October 1927: pp281-282.

Sjogren, Oscar W., "Tractor Testing in Nebraska," *Agricultural Engineering*, February 1921: pp34-37.

"Small Farmer Will Have Small Tractors to Fit," *Business Week*, October 12, 1932: pp8.

Smith, C. W., "A Study of Users' Experiences with Rubber-Tired Farm Tractors," *Agricultural Engineering*, February 1935: pp45-52.

"The General Purpose Tractor," *Agricultural Engineering*, May 1929: pp178.

"The John Deere General Purpose Wide-Tread Series 'P'," *Two-Cylinder Collector Series*, Volume 1, Two-Cylinder Club, 1991: pp42-63.

"The New John Deere General Purpose Tractors," *Farm Implement News*, December 6, 1934: pp18, 23.

"The Tractors Are Running Hot," *Business Week*, July 15, 1939: pp17-18.

"Tractor Production and Sales," *Farm Implement News*, July 2, 1931: pp21.

"Tractor Production Figures," *Farm Implement News*, March 3, 1932: pp15.

"Tractors on Farms," *Farm Implement News*, May 29, 1930: pp10.

"Tractors on Farms Increase Despite Depression," *Farm Implement News*, August 1, 1935: pp14.

"Tractors on Rubber," *Business Week*, November 30, 1935: pp25-26.

"Tractors on United States Farms," *Farm Implement News*, May 21, 1936: pp20.

"Tractors Outwear Farmers," *Agricultural Engineering*, July 1945: pp275.

"Tractors Triumphant," *Time*, October 28, 1935: pp61-62.

"U.S. Farms by Sizes," *Farm Implement News*, November 19, 1936: pp15.

"What of the Air Tire in 1935?" *Farm Implement News*, February 14, 1935: pp26.

Wileman, R. H., "Pneumatic Tires vs. Steel Wheels for Tractors," *Agricultural Engineering*, February 1934: pp62-63.

Wirt, F. A., "The General Purpose Farm Tractor," *Agricultural Engineering*, May 1924: pp192-194.

Worthington, Wayne, "The Engineer's History of the Farm Tractor," *Implement & Tractor*, January 21, 1967: pp34-35, 43.

Worthington, Wayne, "Engineer's History of the Farm, Tractor II: World War I: Confusion, Development," *Implement & Tractor*, February 7, 1967: pp33, 56.

Worthington, Wayne, "Engineer's Tractor History: The 1920's: Eliminating and Consolidating," *Implement & Tractor*, February 21, 1967: pp46, 73-74.

Worthington, Wayne, "Engineer's Tractor History: Depression and Recovery–Rubber Tires, Fuel, Ferguson," *Implement & Tractor*, March 7, 1967: pp44-45, 63-64.

Worthington, Wayne, "Engineer's Farm History, V: Post-War Standards Progress–and the Beginning of the

Businessman Farmer," *Implement & Tractor,* March 21, 1967: pp34-37.

Worthington, Wayne, "The Engineer's Tractor History: . . . 'We Engineers are Involved in Humanity . . .'," *Implement & Tractor,* May 7, 1967: pp38-39, 62-63.

Zelle, William C., "What Form Will the Tractor Ultimately Take," *Agricultural Engineering,* February 1920: pp35-41.

Zink, W. Leland, "Standardization of the Power Take-Off for Farm Tractors," *Agricultural Engineering,* February 1930: pp75.

Pamphlets, Brochures, and Manuals

Deere and Company, *For Every Farm, for Every Crop, for Every Purpose a John Deere Tractor,* Moline, IL: John Deere sales brochure, 1936.

Deere and Company, *Great John Deere Tractors,* Moline, IL: John Deere sales catalog, 1940.

Deere and Company, *John Deere General Purpose Tractors (Models A and B),* Moline, IL: John Deere sales catalog, 1936.

Deere and Company, *John Deere Models "L" and "LA" Tractors,* Moline, IL: John Deere sales catalog, 1941.

Deere and Company, *Service Manual for John Deere Tractors and Engines: Models D and GP,* Moline, IL.

Deere and Company, *Power Farming with Greater Profit,* Moline, IL: John Deere sales catalog, 1937.

Deere and Company, *The Model B Tractor Joins the Parade of New John Deere Equipment,* Moline, IL: John Deere sales brochure, 1934.

Government Publications

Bureau of Census, Department of Commerce, Statistical Abstract of the United States, 1889, Washington: Government Printing Office, 1889.

Bureau of Census, Department of Commerce, Statistical Abstract of the United States, 1937, Washington: Government Printing Office, 1939.

Federal Trade Commission, Report of the Federal Trade Commission of the Causes of High Prices of Farm Implements, Washington: Government Printing Office, 1920.

Federal Trade Commission, Report of the Agricultural Implement and Machinery Industry: Concentration and Competitive Methods, Washington: Government Printing Office, 1938.

United States Department of Agriculture, Monthly Crop Reporter, Washington: Government Printing Office, July 1920.

United States Department of Agriculture, Power and Machinery in Agriculture, Miscellaneous Publication 107, Washington: Government Printing Office, 1933.

Two-Cylinder Club Publications

"John Deere Tractor Identification Part I—Models A, B, C, D & GP," *Two-Cylinder,* November-December 1991: pp2-25.

"John Deere Tractor Identification Part II—Models G, H, R, M, & L Series," *Two-Cylinder,* January-February 1992: pp2-20.

"Model G Tractor (Unstyled)," *Two-Cylinder,* September-October 1989: pp2-18.

"The John Deere Model B (Unstyled)," *Two-Cylinder,* July-August 1991: pp2-21.

"The John Deere Model B (Unstyled) Part II," *Two-Cylinder,* September-October 1991: pp2-20.

"The John Deere Model G (Styled)," *Two-Cylinder,* May-June 1992: pp1-7.

Index